MW01595031

A Christian Woman's Realm

From Birth to Death

Elaine Michele Fipps

Faithful Life Publishers
North Fort Myers, FL
FaithfulLifePublishers.com

A Christian Woman's Realm ~ From Birth to Death

Copyright © 2014 Elaine Michele Fipps
ISBN: 978-1-63073-047-5

Published and printed by:
Faithful Life Publishers
North Fort Myers, FL   33903

888.720.0950

www.FaithfulLifePublishers.com
info@FaithfulLifePublishers.com

Bible quotes are taken from the King James Version.

19 18 17 16 15 14   1 2 3 4 5

Table of Contents

Acknowledgements

*I thank the Lord for leading and helping me
to write this study guide.*

I thank those who reviewed this text:
Mrs. Rebecca Barnes
Mrs. Maria Betts
Pastor and Mrs. Wade Bostic
Mrs. Jennie Butler
Miss Monica Jackson
Mrs. Karen Powell

*A special thanks to Mrs. Dawn Phillips
for reviewing and editing this text.*

*A special thanks to the Victory Baptist Church
(James Island, SC) ladies' Bible study group,
who sat under the teaching of this
material for eight weeks.*

Introduction

The world system today is not a friend of women. The boundary lines for the roles of men and women in society have long been blurred and will continue to worsen as we draw to the end of time. Women are taxed with building careers while taking care of their husband, children, and home. The perfect home with the pretty white picket fence, children dressed in designer clothes, and a powerful corporate position are the **status quo** goals for women to achieve. All the while, the medicine cabinets are lined with stress-related remedies.

Unfortunately, this scenario is playing out in the lives of Christian and non-Christian women alike. However, God has a plan for the Christian woman that differs from the world. When a woman follows God's plan, she will find peace and joy that she will never get from the world. A peace and joy that really cannot be explained—only experienced. The **somewhat** perfect home and life are attainable, just attainable in a different way from the worldly method. Lest we forget, perfection is truly found in the eye of the beholder, and not the world looking in. The only one who truly can measure perfection is the creator of it and that is God.

When God created man and woman He made them distinctly different, yet able to function together as one complete unit. The societal trend has been to promote men and women to fill the roles of the other to establish some sort of equality. This also is a means to advance man's method of doing things his own way. Conversely, God never intended either sex to fulfill the role of the other. When an individual part of a unit does not function properly as intended, the entire unit will not function properly.

Society promotes and advances the dysfunctionalism that already exists in sinful man. The inherent nature of sin produces a life that is lived contrary to the will of God. The only help that exists for this problem is a personal relationship with Jesus Christ and the indwelling of the Holy Spirit of God. This relationship helps us to live a life following God's will and plan. *For we are his workmanship, created in Christ Jesus unto good works, which God hath before ordained that we should walk in them.* (Ephesians 2:10)

In God's plan, a Christian female has a role and purpose perfectly designed just for her. When that role is not filled, it produces unrest, dissatisfaction, and no peace. The initial role of a daughter is subject to the responsibility of her parents, until she takes a husband. *Therefore shall a man leave his father and his mother, and shall cleave unto his wife: and they shall be one flesh.* (Genesis 2:24) From the time of birth until she says, "I do," our daughters need Godly, Holy Spirit-led direction, love, and nurturing. As Christian parents, we—not the world—are the primary advocates for our daughters and the ones responsible for her upbringing and care. After marriage, the role of a Christian woman is subject to the authority of her husband.

Titus admonishes that the aged women teach the younger women. *That they may teach the young women to be sober, to love their husbands, to love their children, to be discreet, chaste, keepers at home, good, obedient to their own husbands, that the word of God be not blasphemed.* (Titus 2:4-5) I personally take Titus' admonition seriously as an aged woman. The content of this book is an overview of God's instruction to women in every phase of life from birth to death. Each chapter builds upon the previous one. If a topic does not seem fully developed in one chapter, it will be in the next. The final chapter of this book will reveal a culmination of the Christian woman's life built on all of the principles laid out in the previous chapters. Let us learn much from God's Word about how to properly fill our roles as women. To God be the glory. Amen!

Chapter 1

Little Girls and Little Curls

There has been much debate over what exactly makes a person who they are—their personality, character, and behavior. Is it inherent nature or is it environment and how children are reared? I submit that it is both, nature and nurture. The Scripture says, *For the imagination of man's heart is evil from his youth.* (Genesis 8:21b) *Train up a child in the way he should go.* (Proverbs 22:6a) Nature is a huge factor in human life, because we are all sinners from birth. We understand this when we witness a child's temper and selfishness at the earliest ages. Nurture and environment are the modes that God uses to rein in and control that sinful nature. The Lord God coined the words *nurture* and *nature* before the thought of psychology ever existed.

God gives us clear direction to raise our children in the nurture and admonition of the Lord. *And, ye fathers, provoke not your children to wrath: but bring them up in the nurture and admonition of the Lord.* (Ephesians 6:4) The responsibility for a child could conceivably exist for their entire life. In the early years we are laying down a foundation for them, teaching them good habits and morals. As they grow into adulthood we instruct them with the Word of God, always directing them toward the Lord. Love for the Lord and the well-being of our child are key factors in rearing children. A relationship based on love promotes a desire to obey because of that love. In contrast, a rule and compliance-driven relationship promotes rebellion.

From birth until around one year of life parents are basically providing love, security, and daily needs for their child. This is an important time of bonding. During this time, children learn their environment and surroundings. From the first year to about the fifth year will be the most intense training time. It is during this time that the male and female differences begin to show; such as the moodiness of girls and their methods of getting what they want. Biblical child rearing techniques can be generalized with boys and girls at a very young age, but certainly become more gender specific as your child grows.

I have loved the following poem since I was a young girl, before I was even saved. It reveals an important truth as we build the life of our child.

The Builder

A builder builded a temple.
He wrought it with grace and skill;
Pillars, [hedges] and arches
All fashioned to work his will.
Men said, as they saw its beauty,
'It shall never know decay.
Great is thy skill, O Builder!
Thy fame shall endure for aye.'

A teacher builded a temple
With loving and infinite care,
Planning each arch with patience,
Laying each stone with prayer.
None praised her unceasing efforts.
None knew of her wondrous plan,
For the temple the teacher builded
Was unseen by the eyes of man.

Gone is the builder's temple,
Crumbled into the dust.
Low lies each stately pillar,
Food for consuming rust.
But the temple the teacher builded
Will last while the ages roll,
For that beautiful unseen temple
Was a child's immortal soul.

Author Unknown

I think of the task of training a young child as building a foundation for life. A building is only as strong as its foundation. As Christians, we know that the foundation of the life of our child needs to be built on Jesus Christ and His Word. *For other foundation can no man lay than that is laid, which is Jesus Christ.* (1 Corinthians 3:11) That which is built upon the rock of Christ will not sink or crumble when the waves of life crash upon it.

The Foundation of the Word

Therefore shall ye lay up these words in your heart and in your soul, and bind them for a sign upon your hand, that they may be as frontlets between your eyes. And ye shall teach them your children, speaking of them when thou sittest in thine house, and when thou walkest by the way, when thou liest down, and when thou risest up. (Deuteronomy 11:18-19)

The sustenance that every person needs is God in their lives. We know God and understand Him and His desire for our lives through His Word. First and foremost, our children need the Word of God. As we teach the Word of God to them, we also need to live it before them, through every part of our life as Deuteronomy 11:18-19 indicates. A parent who walks contrary to what they teach or ignores the principles they teach, will make them valueless and without meaning to their children. God forbid that we make His Word of no value in the eyes of our children.

God's Word contains the path to life, blessings, and protection. It shows us how to live and what we should and should not do. God's Word is the power in our lives for salvation and for Christian living. The Apostle Paul said, *For I am not ashamed of the gospel of Christ: for it is the power of God unto salvation to everyone that believeth; to the Jew first, and also to the Greek.* (Romans 1:16) God's Word will speak to us personally, pointing out sin and areas in our life that need to change.

It is our responsibility as parents, to introduce the Word of God into the lives of our children. We can instill the Word of God at the earliest ages by reading it to them. As they grow, our children can learn the Word through Scripture memory. Choose verses that would be helpful to the child and break them down in length that is age appropriate. Work on the verse for a couple of weeks, going over the verse often each day. Some suggested memory verses: Ephesians 6:1, Proverbs 20:11, Psalm 56:3, and the Ten Commandments in Exodus 20. Memorizing the verses is not enough; children need to know how to apply the verses to everyday life. This helps it become real to them and it will stay with them. Knowing and not doing is of no benefit. *Therefore to him that knoweth to do good, and doeth it not, to him it is sin.* (James 4:17)

Family devotions are a very good way to teach the Word and apply it to everyday life. There are books that can be used to teach Bible stories and daily devotions. Another way is to teach Bible stories straight from our Bible. If using a Bible story book, we always should have our Bible open on the table or in our lap, so our child knows that what is taught comes from God's Word. Be sure that supplemental books are scripturally correct and align with personal biblical beliefs. Children's Bible songs and hymns are another good way to teach the Word of God. Children love to sing and the songs stay with them. Folks lead busy lives today, but we should have family devotions as often as we can. If it seems difficult to get into a pattern, keep trying; do not give up.

Our attitude toward the Word of God will flow over to our child. A child's first impressions of God are formulated in their view of their parents. We live in a day where the Word of God is denied and Christians are turning from the Word to men's opinions. It is vitally important to teach our children God's Word, how to apply it, and how to discern truth from error. *All scripture is given by inspiration of God, and is profitable for doctrine, for reproof, for correction, for instruction in righteousness: that the man of God may be perfect, thoroughly furnished unto all good works.* (2 Timothy 3:16-17)

A young child is likened to an immature tree in the Scripture. As a tree matures and grows, its root system grows. Scientists have developed a method with infrared cameras, by which they can video a tree's root system during storms. The information gleaned from the videos has a very good scriptural application. What scientists found was that during storms, the root system of certain trees actually moves to dig deeper and grip into the soil, as if to hold on to withstand the storm. When we build our children's lives on the Word of God, their foundations and roots will be strong. When storms arise, our children's roots (just like trees) will stretch forth deeper to grasp and hold onto the things they have learned in the Word of God. *Therefore whosoever heareth these sayings of mine, and doeth them, I will liken him unto a wise man, which built his house upon a rock: and the rain descended, and the floods came, and the winds blew, and beat upon that house; and it fell not: for it was founded upon a rock.* (Matthew 7:24-25)

There is a special promise given to those who train a child in God's Word. *When he is old, he will not depart from it.* (Proverbs 22:6b) The way that a child should go is toward God, by the way of His Word. *Strong's Concordance* defines the word train as *to narrow or to initiate or discipline.* We associate training with competition, preparing for a job, or learning a skill. One thing that is needed in training is consistency. No one trains to excel at anything in life in a short period of time. So goes training a child—it is a task that starts at birth and continues on through life. It is a continual, repetitive process. Proverbs 22:6b does not say that the child will never rebel or stray or go away from God's path for his or her life. However, it does promise that when they are old they will not depart from their training. This reminds me of the old saying, *the chickens always come home to roost.* Every follower of Christ, more than once, goes off of God's path somewhere along the way in their lives. The important thing is that they come back to the path.

God reveals so much truth in nature and includes examples in His Word. *The ants are a people not strong, yet they prepare their meat in the summer; the conies are but a feeble folk, yet make they their houses in the rocks.* (Proverbs 30:25-26) The salmon fish amaze me with their pattern of birth, travel, and then their return back to the exact place of birth to spawn and die. In the travel of the salmon, some are lost to death along the way. Unfortunately, some children who stray are lost in death along the way, but the Word of God is never invalid. God placed in salmon the innate sense to follow their life pattern; He does much more for human life. We as parents, with God's help and His Word, place in our children the sense to follow the Lord. There is no perfect parent, except the Lord; we do our best and leave the rest to Him.

I have heard it said (and I agree) that following rules (as in God's rules) without having a relationship leads to rebellion. The relationship here can apply two ways: parent to child and child to God. The relationship of a parent to a child is so very important. We need to love our children with a Godly love. Some children are easier to love than others, but all need love. Godly love is unconditional, merciful, and always looking out for the best interest of the child. Training and discipline done with Godly love is so much sweeter and easier to be entreated. Your child also needs to learn to love God for who He is and what He has done for us, which is revealed in His Word. If we love God as we should, it will be easy to teach our children to love Him.

The most important result of teaching your child God's Word is that it reveals sin to them and their need for salvation. *So then faith cometh by hearing, and hearing by the word of God.* (Romans 10:17) Salvation should be our heart's desire for our children. Paul wrote to Timothy: *And that from a child thou hast known the Holy Scriptures, which are able to make thee wise unto salvation through faith which is in Christ Jesus.* (2 Timothy 3:15) Do not ever underestimate the power of the Word of God. *For the word of God is quick, and powerful, and sharper than any two-edged sword, piercing even to the dividing asunder of soul and spirit, and of the joints and marrow, and is a discerner of the thoughts and intents of the heart.* (Hebrews 4:12)

The following sections discuss character traits that we develop and build on the Word of God in the lives of our children.

Obedience

Obedience is the most basic quality we can teach our children. *Encarta Dictionary* defines obedience as *the act or practice of following instructions, complying with rules or regulations, or submitting to somebody's authority.* Obedience is simply obeying a command that has been given and is the basic foundation for our entire Christian life. Children are commanded to obey their parents. *Children, obey your parents in the Lord for this is right.* (Ephesians 6:1) Children who become Christians are to obey the Lord. *Ye shall walk after the Lord your God, and fear him, and keep his commandments, and obey his voice, and ye shall serve him, and cleave unto him.* (Deuteronomy 13:4) Servants are to obey their masters and citizens are to obey the authority over them. The Scriptures are filled with directions that demand obedience.

God's Word is the foundation for the Christian life; obedience is the first building block, as we build our lives through Christ. A child that is taught to obey from a young age has less difficulty obeying God in their lives when they come to know Him. For a woman this matter of obedience is especially important, because she has a two-tier chain of command when she marries—the Lord and then her husband. *For the husband is the head of the wife, even as Christ is the head of the church: and he is the Savior of the body.* (Ephesians 5:23) It is important to also remember that obedience leads to blessings and provisions. *A blessing, if ye obey the commandments of the Lord your God, which I (Moses) command you this day: and a curse, if ye will not obey the commandments of the Lord your God, but turn aside out of the way which I command you this day, to go after other gods, which ye have not known.* (Deuteronomy 11:27-28)

A very important part of obedience is doing it immediately. The word immediately means just what the word implies: *instantly, right away, and without delay.* Delayed obedience is not real obedience at all, because hesitation is initially disobedience. Immediate obedience is such an important factor for a child; in some situations it could be a life or death factor. I remember a story that a mother told concerning her family living in the desert. Their backyard bordered on a huge desert area that was overrun with scorpions. One day she noticed her child walking toward a large scorpion at the edge of the yard. She told the child to stop; the child immediately stopped, because she had taught the child to do so. That child was spared from harm, because they were trained to obey immediately.

It is not an easy task to teach children to obey. It takes a tremendous amount of time and effort to teach obedience. The process is often very frustrating and tiring, but it is well worth it for the child. Actually, it is also well worth it for the parent, because the parent will reap benefit from it in the future. I have often seen and heard parents use the multiple chance method of teaching obedience: "Jill, this is your second warning to get out of bed for school!" I was watching my grandchildren one day. My grandson got upset and threw his mother's iPad across the floor. We both moved to get the iPad and when I got it first, he hit me. I immediately picked him up, without a word, and dealt with the problem. Afterwards, I told him that I loved him, but that he could never hit me, his mom, or his dad—ever. Issues of direct disobedience, rebellion, acts of hatred, and violence need swift attention.

But a rod is for the back of him that is void of understanding. (Proverbs 10:13b) *Withhold not correction from the child: for if thou beatest him with the rod, he shall not die. Thou shalt beat him with the rod, and shall deliver his soul from Hell.* (Proverbs 23:13-14) I know that society, in general, is against corporal punishment or spanking. Who will we believe—God or the world? I personally hated spanking my children and probably did not do it as often as I should have. Spanking my grandchildren is even more difficult than my children! Spanking is not abuse when it is done properly and in a loving manner. When we touch a hot stove we get an immediate rebuttal with a burnt finger or hand, which teaches us not to touch the stove again. The point here is that there needs to be immediate consequences for disobedience; then as the child grows the moments of hesitation to obey will decline.

Spanking and discipline really display a great love for our children and their well-being. Teaching your child to obey you will carry over to your child obeying the Lord. Some children are stronger-willed than others. Never give up on your child. It may take some time to see improvement. Remain faithful to the task of discipline. *The father of the righteous shall greatly rejoice: and he that begetteth a wise child shall have joy of him. Thy father and thy mother shall be glad, and she that bare thee shall rejoice.* (Proverbs 23:24-25) The word begetteth means *to birth a child*, but it also means to bring up the child.

Non-Controlling

One characteristic that can be found in most little girls is the desire to control and lead others. God's intended chain of command is

Himself, men, and then women. When little boys control and lead, it is not as noticeable as when little girls do the same. There is a difference in trying to control your own destiny and the lives of others, as opposed to exercising a God-given place of authority. We often say that little girls are bossy, but the root of the issue is a desire to control.

The desire to control one's own life and go our own way is rebellion against God. *Encarta Dictionary* defines rebellion as *the opposition to or defiance of authority*. God is the only and final authority of the entire universe. Pride, the root of all sin, causes us to rebel; and rebellion against God and His commands is the definition of sin. When King Saul did not follow God's Word in taking the spoil of the enemy, Samuel told him, *For rebellion is as the sin of witchcraft, and stubbornness is as iniquity and idolatry. Because thou has rejected the word of the Lord, he hath also rejected thee from being king.* (1 Samuel 15:23)

When Eve took of the fruit in the garden, her action opposed (or rebelled) against God's authority in her life and rejected His spoken Word. Now, because of the events in the Garden of Eden, we all have a sin nature. The nature to sin is within us, but we can refuse to grow those sinful desires with the Lord's help. I know that rebellious desire resides in me and I can only suppress it with the Lord's help.

I have witnessed the desire of control in the lives of many Christian women today. The world fosters that idea and provides an environment conducive to its growth. Watch and listen to your daughter as she interacts with her siblings and others. When you observe that tendency to control others and situations, you need to talk with her. Carefully explain what should change about her behavior. It is very wise to think through your explanation, before you have to apply them to her situation. Your child's age always determine your actions. It may be appropriate to remove her from the situation she is trying to control. As she grows, you may have her apologize to others for her controlling actions. If she is trying to manipulate to gain something she wants or to participate in an activity, withhold those from her. Parenting takes time, determination, and fortitude, but you will never regret your efforts. We will only regret those things we failed to do.

There are times and situations where women are to lead, such as in a ladies' Bible study or in a Sunday school class. For a woman, submissive leadership can be a very fine line against controlling authority. When people lead, they show others the way and go before them, which is not the same as being in authority. Most of us would use Deborah, a prophetess and judge in the Scriptures, as an example of a woman leader. However, Deborah never exercised authority or control over Israel; she only gave forth the Word and discerned between right and wrong (see Judges 4).

Often in ladies Bible studies, we focus on the God-fearing, faithful women of the Bible as examples on how we ought to live. However, some important lessons can be gleaned from the evil women depicted in Scriptures. Every time I hear the name Jezebel, I think of a loose woman. Conversely, Jezebel was actually a very controlling woman who ruled her home. When Jezebel's husband was distraught over not getting the land he wanted, Jezebel told him, *Dost thou not govern the kingdom of Israel? Arise, and eat bread, and let thine heart be merry: I will give thee the vineyard of Naboth the Jezereelite.* (1 Kings 21:7) Jezebel did exactly that. She took matters into her own hands and got the vineyard for Ahab by very evil means.

How often have I seen women, myself included, step in and try to control situations to attain something or some outcome they desired. That is indeed the spirit of Jezebel. At the end of the lives of Ahab and Jezebel, the Scriptures say this—*But there was none like unto Ahab, which did sell himself to work wickedness in the sight of the Lord, whom Jezebel his wife stirred up.* (1 Kings 21:25) Of all the kings of Israel and Judah, only one wife was mentioned as *stirring up* her husband and that was Jezebel. Oh, may it never be said of us or our daughters that we were controlling our husbands, provoking them to do evil!

Self-Control

The next area of focus for our daughter is learning how to control emotions and actions. As she ages and matures, the ability to control her emotions and actions will strengthen. It is our job as mothers to work on self-control as early as possible. Even a child can possess his or her vessel in a pleasing manner. I was in our church fellowship hall one Sunday evening waiting for the choir to assemble, when I observed an interesting scene. Two girls, approximately eight or nine years old, were chasing a boy their age. The lead girl was so close to catching the young man that when he suddenly stopped, she ran into him and started flailing to catch herself. The boy looked at her and said, "You better get a hold of yourself." I had to laugh when I thought that even this young boy knew the girl's actions were out of control. Children need to have a childhood and have fun as children, but even in the early years girls need to know how to possess their vessels properly.

If you are a Christian parent you should be training your children to be Christians even before they are saved. *That every one of you should know how to possess his vessel in sanctification and honour.* (1 Thessalonians 4:4) Have you ever thought about the fact that our children are apprentice Christians? An apprentice is one who is being prepared or trained to be a skilled craftsman or journeyman. Our daughters need to know how to live the Christian life before they become Christians, so they will be better prepared. Many of us know people who were not raised in a Christian home and saved later in life. Those people tend to be rough around the edges until they mature spiritually, which often takes a long time. I know this truth very well, for such was my case.

What does it mean to possess our vessel? The word possess is used three times in the New Testament and all three times the word has the same meaning. According to *Strong's Concordance*, the word possess has a very simple meaning: *to own or possess*. If we have ownership and possession of something, then we have control over how the item is used and what it does. For example, if we own a dog or cat, do we allow that animal to run wild as we possess it or do we train it and keep in under control? The same goes with our physical human bodies. Do we let ourselves go wild and unrestrained, or do we control ourselves and come into subjection to the Word of God? *In sanctification and honour* means (according to *Strong's Concordance*) *to hold in a state of purity, holiness, and high esteem*. This admonition sounds pretty mature for a child, but we have to start somewhere with this matter of control, and it starts at childhood. A green twig is much more pliable than a mature tree!

I cannot state this often enough—watch and listen to your daughters! When she exhibits a lack of self-control, speak with her. Tell her specifically what she has done in age-appropriate language. Be careful to discern between a true lack of self-control versus childish behavior. If our daughter throws a fit when she is tired, we first need to be sure that we have not contributed to her dilemma. As a parent we always need to be contemplating and considering the environment and situations for our families.

When my children were young, I would plan my day always considering how it would affect everyone else. I still plan my days that way, considering interruption in meals and sleep patterns and try to make the impact as minimal as possible. Plan accordingly. Obviously there will be times of unscheduled turmoil and interruptions. How we handle those times will have a direct influence on our children. As a child grows, they need to understand that they should exhibit good behavior and self-control at all times no matter the situation.

In general, the majority of people put their best appearances on in public, then let their hair down at home. Most certainly there are things we may do at home that we would not do in public, such as dressing comfortably, cutting up, and acting silly. However, a Christian is and should be a Christian 24/7, not just out in public. It is not good for our children to get the impression that they can display bad behavior at home and good behavior in public. This will send mixed signals to our kids.

The main place of learning and practicing self-control is at home. Our homes are the greenhouse for the soil that our children grow in. The individuals that make up society are a product of homes. Our Christian homes need to produce godly young people that live and show forth the Word of God. If our child throws a tantrum and exhibits uncontrolled behavior at home or in public, handle the situation immediately. Remove the child to a place of solitude until they gain control of themselves. When my daughter would throw a tantrum at home I would walk away and leave her, which was not the best way to handle the situation. The cause of the tantrum, the continuance of the problem, and the age of the child will determine further action, such as corporal punishment or restrictions.

When Titus instructs the older women to teach the younger he says it is so *that the word of God be not blasphemed.* (Titus 2:5b) The word blasphemed in this context means *to defame, rail on, or speak evil of.* The unsaved are always looking to derail God's Word or make it of no effect so that it does not condemn their lives. Uncontrolled behavior from a person who professes to be saved derails God's Word.

Contentment

I have heard Dr. Ron Comfort speak many times. He is a wonderful expositor of God's Word. Dr. Comfort is father to three daughters. He has often said that while raising his girls he had to tell them at certain times, "Stop crying or I will give you something to cry about." I heard that statement myself in my early years. Most of us can understand why that comment is so necessary. Girls frequently cry more than boys. There is a tendency for little girls to cry and whine over the smallest thing and sometimes over everything, but it ought not to be so. Little girls who cry often are frustrating— big girls and women that cry often are intolerable. Children know how and when to cry from birth. Crying is initially a child's way of communicating: "I am hungry." "I am wet." or "I am in pain." However, as a child grows, crying for other reasons, such as anger, unhappiness, wanting their way, or wanting attention, gets added to the mix. These are some of the reasons little girls continue to use crying.

My daughter cried or pouted every day of her life until her teen years. I did not come to know the Lord until she was five years old and I did not handle her childhood issues very well. A good portion of a child's character is built by the time they are five. She would get upset about something and go sit under our dining room table. I used to go sit with her and tell her that she would have a hard life, if she got upset about everything. I would say, "Don't kick against the pricks," which comes from Acts 9 and the conversion of the Apostle Paul. A prick is a *sharp point or a goad used to prod animals in a certain direction*. Training and discipline can be a goad to a child. When a child fights against training, discipline, and the realities of life, they will not be happy about it. Crying and pouting worsens every situation and the child's outlook. We as parents have to end that tendency to cry and pout over everything.

Many times we take the easy route by doing everything we can to rectify whatever the child is crying about, to make them stop. However, they have to learn to deal with whatever is triggering the crying. Often when my daughter would cry about not getting her way, I would just walk away and leave her. I did not give her any attention. A better solution would have been to talk to her, in a calm voice, about why she was crying, explain why she should not be crying, and then place her in solitude. As she grew, I did talk to her about what she was crying about and address those issues with her. We have to teach an alternative to crying, which is how to deal with life situations. When my children were young, I was *the blind leading the blind* as I matured in Christ. I made many mistakes. Thank the Lord, He helps us with our many failures when we are trying to do things His way.

A primary cause of unnecessary crying is discontentment. In 1 Timothy 6, Paul talks about contentment when he tells Timothy to withdraw from men that *suppose that gain is godliness.* He then goes on to say, *but godliness with contentment is great gain. For we brought nothing into this world, and it is certain we can carry nothing out. And having food and raiment let us be therewith content* (1 Timothy 6:6-8). The word contentment is only used this one time in Scripture and it means *self-satisfaction.* When the Apostle Paul says, *for I have learned, in whatsoever state I am, therewith to be content* (Philippians 4:11b), the word content here means *self-complacent.* The word self-complacent means *content and satisfied.*

A good percentage of our attitude in life comes from our outlook on life. Talk to your daughter about situations that arise and give place to discontentment. Give her an alternative view—God's view from His Word. If your daughter has shelter, food, clothing, and is in no pain, she has nothing to cry or pout about. Scripture memory would work well for this and would help to remind her when these situations arise. Discontentment breeds a myriad of sins and problems in this very materialistic world we live in. Content children become content adults. My grandmother reached the ripe age of 100 last year. One quality I admire in her is that of always be content, no matter her situation.

We cannot really discuss discontentment without discussing jealously. Jealously breeds in situations where we feel that things are not fair to us. If we take our eyes off of the Lord and put them on the world, we will feel that life is not fair every day of our lives. When we are not thankful or lack gratitude to God in our lives, jealousy will increase. The most important thing to know about judging the fairness of the situations in our lives is to understand our God. Our God is the only perfect Father. God knows us thoroughly because He created us; He knows our lives and what we need.

It is an awesome thought to realize that God is sovereign and controls the entire universe and orchestrates the paths of our lives. Our children need to understand that when a family or an individual is in the will of God and walking the path that He has for them, God gives what is best for them. Only God knows the plan that will produce the best results. Good or bad, God has a purpose and plan in everything. We can make choices and take actions outside of God's will, but everything that comes into our lives has passed through the will of God. Remember the story of Job; Satan could not do anything in Job's life without God's permission. *And the Lord said unto Satan, Behold, all that he hath is in thy power; only upon himself put not thine hand. So Satan went forth from the presence of the Lord.* (Job 1:12)

As Christians *we know that all things work together for good to them that love God, to them who are the called according to his purpose.* (Romans 8:28) Children need to learn from a young age not to murmur and complain about life or be jealous of others and their situations. All murmuring and complaining is against God and is a serious matter. *And in the morning, then ye shall see the glory of the Lord; for that he heareth your murmurings against the Lord.* (Exodus 16:7a) *Neither murmur ye, as some of them also murmured, and were destroyed of the destroyer.* (1 Corinthians 10:10)

Deter a Busybody

One thing that can stimulate jealously and complaining is increased knowledge of the lives of others. Today with the popularity of social media, an enormous amount of private and personal information is available. Our curiosity is fed continually, but never satisfied. Some older Christians avoid sites such as Facebook, because they fear the loss of privacy. Recently a brother in Christ told me and another lady that his wife did not want him to go on Facebook, because all of his business would be all over the world. She is very correct, but only to the extent that we put our business on Facebook.

A good way to use Facebook is to keep up with people, especially our grown children. Watching what people post is a good indicator of where people are spiritually and can also indicate when someone is headed down the wrong path. As Christians, we are responsible for each other and should not judge, but rather step in and help when we see the need. As parents, we should stay connected into the lives of our children, because we are parents for their entire lives.

Social media, unfortunately, leaves few stones unturned and drives people to want to know anything and everything about others. In the days before the internet and social media, we would label people a busybody if they displayed such a need to know everything. In 1 Peter 4, Peter talks about Christians bearing reproach for the name of Christ. He says if we bear reproach, *let none of you suffer as a murderer, or as a thief, or as an evildoer, or as a busybody in other men's matters.* (1 Peter 4:15) It is very interesting that being a busybody is listed with murder and thievery.

The term busybody means more than being nosey about other people's business. It also means to know the business of others and to tell it or blab it. Think about it this way, when we know information about others and we tell it, we can murder a person's character and testimony before the world. When we tell information about others, we steal their privacy. When we tell information about others, we can separate friends. *A forward man soweth strife: and a whisperer separateth chief friends.* (Proverbs 16:28) When we tell information about others, we can be perceived by the world as an evil doer. Need I say more?

Recently a group was waiting at church to assemble to go to an event. A lady asked if a particular family was coming. She was told that the family was showing their home to be rented and they would arrive soon. As the family came in the door that lady went up and said, "How did your rental showing go?" The look on the face of the husband said it all—*how in the world did you know that?* Today, everything we say can and will be repeated and possibly used against us. It is best to be a woman of few words, and *let your yea be yea; and your nay, nay; lest ye fall into condemnation.* (James 5:12b) Be a person of your word and let your words be few!

You may be wondering what all of this has to do with training our daughters. First of all, we set the example for our daughters in this matter of knowing the business of others. Children, who live in homes where discussing the business of others is common occurrence, will not see any wrong or harm in the practice. They will carry the practice on into their own homes. *Death and life are in the power of the tongue: and they that love it shall eat the fruit thereof.* (Proverbs 18:21) We need to examine the sentence to understand this verse. *They that love it,* refers back to *the power of the tongue.* They that love the power of the tongue shall eat the fruit of it. So exactly what is the power of the tongue?

Even so the tongue is a little member, and boasteth great things. Behold, how great a matter a little fire kindleth! And the tongue is a fire, a world of iniquity: so is the tongue among our members, that it defileth the whole body, and setteth on fire the course of nature; and it is set on fire of hell. (James 3:5-6)

What great power the tongue has to be able to set on fire the course of nature! When our daughters are privy to unnecessary information, it can cause all types of emotional responses and thoughts that often they are too immature to deal with. Lest we forget, most times we never know the whole story of the situation of others we are repeating; only God does. In my days as a child, adults did not discuss sensitive matters in front of children (their own or others), which is not the case today. A child's mind takes information in literally and cannot fill in the missing parts with intuition they do not have.

Finally, a child can fear that what is happening in another home can happen in theirs. There is always certain, filtered information that for various reasons a child needs to know, but the majority of the time they are taking in a lot that they never needed to hear.

Keep Them a Busy Body

One of my favorite secular songs, *Coal Miner's Daughter*, was written in 1969 by Loretta Lynn about her life. My children still laugh at me today if they hear the song. One line in the song says, *The work we done was hard, at night we'd sleep 'cause we were tired.* That line reminds me of the old days and especially of farming families. Children always had to work and help on a farm. There were chores that had to be done and everyone had to participate. Some good results of this were that children learned good work ethics, team work, got into less trouble, and were not in front of the television.

Whether you live on a farm or in the city, keeping children busy is a good thing. *Slothfulness casteth into a deep sleep; and an idle soul shall suffer hunger.* (Proverbs 19:15) Children today do not know the rigors of hard work. We have become a soft society. *Behold, this was the iniquity of thy sister Sodom, pride, fullness of bread, and **abundance of idleness** was in her and in her daughters, neither did she strengthen the hand of the poor and needy.* (Ezekiel 16:49) I do agree with the statement, idle hands are the devil's workshop. I know in my own life, when I am idle I tend to stray from the Lord quicker. There are an abundance of worldly activities, which are not necessarily sinful, that pull us away from the Lord.

Some may think it harsh to make children work and do chores. However, they are not reasoning out the good benefits for the child. Picking up clothes, making beds, and putting away toys teaches children order and cleanliness. Raking leaves, mowing grass, pulling weeds, and picking up trash gets them into the fresh air, away from the television and video games, and helps their bodies rest well at night. Doing dishes, taking out the trash, dusting the furniture, sweeping, and vacuuming teaches them they are part of a team and that families work together. The types of chores a child can do are endless. Putting together chores that are done on a schedule helps a child learn to be punctual and responsible. Remember there is no such thing as *woman's work*. It is okay for girls and boys to do the same types of chores. Our daughters could be in a remote foreign mission field one day and have to do things most women would not. We would be glad that she was prepared.

Doing chores is not just preparation for the mission field; it is preparation for normal daily life. Most children will probably not be happy about doing chores (many adults are not either), but be persistent and make it a requirement. Also, try to make chores fun. Do the chores with them. Sing while you work. Our attitude toward chores will flow over to our children. When they are little they love to help; take advantage of that time in life and start with the chores. My grandson, Liam, loves to help rinse the dishes as we wash. We do get wet, but we have fun. It teaches him that we are a family and we all help with the chores. Keeping children busy is a benefit we never fully understand, until it is far too late to start it.

Work is the path to meeting daily needs and receiving reward. Boaz told Ruth after she worked in the fields to take care of her mother-in-law: *The Lord recompense thy work, and a full reward be given thee of the Lord God of Israel, under whose wings thou art come to trust.* (Ruth 2:12) According to *Strong's Concordance*, recompense in this verse means *to be safe in mind, body, or estate.* Our children will be thankful one day that we taught them to work.

Good Speech

Over a period of time we can tell a lot about a woman by her speech. Jesus said to the Pharisees: *O generation of vipers, how can ye, being evil, speak good things? For out of the abundance of the heart the mouth speaketh.* (Matthew 12:34) I said *over a period of time*, because anyone can impress or fool others for a short period of time. However, what is in the heart of a woman will eventually be revealed in her speech and her actions.

Children naturally come out of the womb crying; but obviously, not talking. The majority of what a child learns about speech is learned in the home. It is very important to teach our daughter good speech. I use the term *good speech* to mean: use of proper English and grammar; speech clear to understand; words that are easily received; kind and truthful speech. To teach good speech we have to instruct in the mechanics of speech. More importantly, we have to aim at the heart of the issue of producing proper speech. Good use of grammar, proper English, and clarity issues are purely mechanical and just need to be taught. Listen to your daughter talk; think about her grammar and use of the English language; determine what needs to be adjusted and gently correct and instruct. Grammar and English corrections could last into her teen years. Also, we need to be careful about our own speech. Children mimic what we do much quicker than what we tell them to do.

Unkind, untruthful, hateful, and worldly words are an entirely different type of speech problem that requires extra attention. These types of speech troubles are sinful and reveal a heart problem. *Keep thy heart with all diligence; for out of it are the issues of life.* (Proverbs 4:23) To correct sinful speech we need to get to the root of the sin. Unkind speech can be a result of pride or anger. Worldly speech can be a result of spending too much time watching the television or with worldly people. Lying or untruthful speech can be a result of trying to obtain something that is desired in a wrong manner or to cover up some other sin. The best way to deal with these issues is to talk to your child when the sinful speech first occurs. Find verses in the Bible that deal with the sin problem and go over them with the child. Memorizing Scripture is a good way to help a child remember when she is doing something sinful. This also helps her combat temptations to use wrong speech.

In my own life I use Scripture memory to help me abstain from sin when I am tempted. This works for our daughters as well. One of the Scriptures I use frequently is found in Proverbs 6:16-19.

These six things doth the Lord hate: yea, seven are an abomination unto Him: A proud look, a lying tongue, and hands that shed innocent blood, an heart that deviseth wicked imaginations, feet that be swift in running to mischief, a false witness that speaketh lies, and he that soweth discord among the brethren.

We need to choose a verse or part of a verse to use with our daughters that is appropriate for their age and comprehension level. If the speech problem persists, more stringent, age-appropriate discipline action needs to be taken. I am still of the opinion that a little soap in the mouth never hurt any child or grandchild!

One final word of caution—it is very easy (especially for unsaved children and adults) to adopt a manner of speech that is deceitful and insincere in order to conform. I have taught various age groups of children at church. Have you ever met a child or adult with **too** perfect speech? I have! Children who have perfect manners, always respond appropriately when asked to do something, and are always respectful of their elders are a rare gem—maybe a little too rare. These types of folk leave you thinking, "Wow, they are too good to be true." Sometimes they **are** too good to be true. The Lord often will give us the sense of a lack of sincerity from our children. Lack of sincerity or the façade of perfection is a warning sign to parents of a heart issue—often an unsaved heart issue. *For the Lord seeth not as man seeth; for man looketh on the outward appearance, but the Lord looketh on the heart.* (1 Samuel 16:7b)

Conclusion

As we move through the next chapters, it will become apparent that the topics we have discussed here are important for a woman's entire life. The principles that we teach our girls from an early age will set the underpinning for who they will become as Christian women.

Please remember how important it is to pray daily for our children, from the time they are conceived until death. Pray specifically for their salvation until they are saved and then for them to seek the Lord and His will daily for their lives. Pray for every aspect of their lives, believing the Lord will answer. *And whatsoever ye shall ask in my name, that will I do, that the Father may be glorified in the Son.* (John 14:13) *And this is the confidence that we have in him, that, if we ask any thing according to his will, he heareth us.* (1 John 5:14)

Chapter 1 Review

1. God gives parents clear direction to raise their children in the nurture and admonition of the Lord. Read Ephesians 6:4. What does admonition mean?

2. At what age should we start training our children for the Lord?

3. What is an apprentice?

4. Every life has a foundation just like a building, what tool should we use to build the foundation of our daughter's life?

5. Name some ways we can teach our daughters the Word of God.

6. What do you feel is the single most important concept we can teach our daughters from the Word of God?

7. Read Proverbs 22:6 and write in your own words what you think this verse means. Is it a sure promise?

8. Ephesians 6:1 tells children to obey their parents. What exactly does it mean to obey?

9. Read 1 Samuel 15:1-24. In verse 22, what is the difference in obeying and sacrificing?

10. Does the Bible instruct parents to spank their children? Can you give a verse to back it up?

11. What was the sin of Jezebel? (See 1 Kings 21, etc.)

12. What does it mean to *possess your vessel?* (See I Thessalonians 4:4)

13. What are some of the reasons children cry?

14. Do you think your daughter can be taught to understand what murmuring and complaining is? At what age?

15. In this world of the internet super highway and social media, is it good that girls *know everything?* Why or why not? (See Ephesians 5:10-13)

16. Can a child be taught to work at a young age? (See Proverbs 19:15) Name one benefit for a child that does household chores.

17. How important are the words that your daughter speaks? (See Matthew 12:34)

18. We know what the Bible teaches about the tongue. At what age do we need to begin to work on the speech of our daughters?

Chapter 2

A Time of Transition

When I was ten years old, my family lived in a pretty rough neighborhood in the north area of Charleston, South Carolina. I will never forget our neighbor, Jenny Lou. She was a feisty little brunette, adorned with makeup and a beehive hairdo, at the ripe old age of thirteen. Jenny was my introduction into teen-hood. The unique eye-opener, for me, was the fact that Jenny was the mother of a baby girl. In the late 60s, teens having babies was not as wide spread as it is today. If the teen years could be described from a teen point of view, the word *eye-opener* would probably be a very appropriate description. These years are a time when children begin to look outward to the world, as opposed to inward to their home and families. It is a time of realization that much exists outside of their secure home environment. Of all the time periods in our lives, it can certainly be the most tumultuous one. It is a time of physical change that causes great anxiety. It is a time of struggling with independence versus parental authority. It is a time of life that I would never want to relive.

I am hard pressed to say whether the teen years are more difficult for the teen or the parent. Having been in both positions, I would say it is equally challenging for both parent and child. However, the advantage for the parent is the fact that they have already come through the teen route. I was unsaved as a teenager and from a non-Christian home; however, I was a Christian during my children's teen years. When children are raised in a Christian home, I think the teen years are easier—especially since we have the Lord to guide and help us.

I have often wondered if the Scriptures ever talk about or address the teen years specifically. In fact, the word *youth* is mentioned 69 times in Scripture. Youth refers to juveniles and young people from childhood to marriage. There are a few passages that appear to describe situations that involved a teenager. In Leviticus 24, the son of an Israelite woman and Egyptian father went out into the camp of Israel, strove in the camp, and committed sin.

And the Israelitish woman's son blasphemed the name of the Lord, and cursed. And they brought him unto Moses: (and his mother's name was Shelomith, the daughter of Dibri, of the tribe of Dan:) And they put in him ward, that the mind of the Lord might be shewed them. And the Lord spake unto Moses, saying, bring forth him that hath cursed without the camp; and let all that heard him lay their hands upon his head, and let all the congregation stone him. (Leviticus 24:11-14)

This story seems very indicative of teen years—going out among the people and striving. The word striving means *to fight or to oppose to obtain something*. Teens often strive to obtain their position as an adult and the material things they see in the world. Cursing can unfortunately be a result of not achieving what one is striving to obtain. This teen not only cursed, he cursed using the Lord's name. Stoning may seem a very harsh punishment for the offender, but blaspheming and cursing the name of God is a very serious offense, then and now. We need to remember that the Lord God Himself handed out this punishment. Unfortunately, cursing and taking God's name in vain is so commonplace today that it does not shock us anymore. The offense and the punishment were serious in this account, which relate another side of the teen years—a time of more serious sin.

The teen years are the bridge to adulthood. It is a difficult time for teens as they leave childhood. There can be a lot of uncertainty as to their position in the family and society and how they fit into the whole scheme of life.

As a parent, we often think that as our child grows and is able to do more for themselves our responsibility lessens. I used to think that my job as a mother would be easier when the children were older and could do more. My line of thinking was completely false. The parenting job is not easier during the teen years, although some of the responsibilities change. All through my children's teen years, I wished they were back in diapers when I could shelter them from the world.

From birth to marriage, raising children is a fulltime job. After marriage, we exchange child rearing for child mentoring. Our children never fully reach a point that they can be totally left to themselves. I have often wondered how the previous statement can be true when they reach full grown adulthood. God reminded me the same applies to our relationship with Him; we always need His involvement in our lives, just as our children need our involvement. *The rod and reproof give wisdom: but a child left to himself bringeth his mother to shame.* (Proverbs 29:15) Our relationship with our children changes as they grow, but there is always a relationship. Yes indeed, the teen years present a whole new set of challenges.

Communication

Our most important communication every day should be with the Lord Jesus Christ. *My voice shalt thou hear in the morning, O Lord; in the morning will I direct my prayer unto thee, and will look up.* (Psalm 5:3) Daily prayer is a key help in our communication with others. I thought about my daily prayer life and how it mimics daily communication with my children. Once we are saved, we have the privilege to come boldly before God and talk to Him. *Let us therefore come boldly unto the throne of grace, that we may obtain mercy, and find grace to help in time of need.* (Hebrews 4:16)

Our children should always have an open door to boldly come to us, just like we do before God.

Just as I pray daily, I need to have daily and regular communication with my children. The more time spent in communication, the closer the relationship. The closer the relationship with our children, the more freedom there will be to discuss anything necessary. In my prayer time I know I can pour out my heart before the Lord without fear of ridicule. Our children should feel the same way in communication with us. When I approach the Lord with a request, I always receive an answer. Our children should always receive an answer from us, although we may not always know or have an answer for them. It is okay to tell them we will find the answer and bring it back to them. The Lord already knows what I need before I approach Him in prayer. We should know our children so intimately that we know their needs as well. I know that the Lord **always** has my best interest at heart, so should it be with our children. The Lord communicates with me through His Word, which is always truth spoken in love. May we exhibit the same with our children!

We discussed in Chapter One the importance of listening to our daughters to help correct their speech and their actions. We also discussed the need to talk to them and explain the areas that need to change in their behavior. Building communication with our children from the ages of one to ten will set the stage for communication during the teen years. Our discussions with our children need to grow to the point that we can discuss anything with them. This is so necessary during the teen years, because they will have a lot of difficult questions and situations to discern.

An important aspect of talking with our teens and our adult children, and really anyone for that matter, is making sure our approach does not include ridicule or anger for unwise choices and decisions. Our speech can often lead to defensive responses and put up a barrier to open communication. *A word fitly spoken is like apples of gold in pictures of silver.* (Proverbs 25:11) The word fitly means *appropriate.* Every person desires to feel loved and accepted. We always need to be certain that our children know we love them and accept them, even when we cannot condone or accept their behavior or actions. We should always pray before talking to our children about sinful behavior. A good prayer can be found in Psalm 19:14: *Let the words of my mouth, and the meditation of my heart, be acceptable in thy sight, O Lord, my strength and my redeemer.*

Along with prayer, a particular practice has helped me with communication over the years. Pastor Herbert O'Neal told me long ago, "Don't accuse, but don't excuse." My understanding of that statement is to never outright accuse of wrong doing during conversations, but do not excuse sinful behavior either. Use the Word of God to point out the sin, because it is the true discerner of sinful behavior and wrong actions. Pointing out what God says about the behavior or situation allows the Word of God to directly accuse and not us. God's Word is the final authority and all sin is first and foremost against Him. *I had not known sin, but by the law: for I had not known lust, except the law had said, Thou shalt not covet.* (Romans 7:7b)

Situations will arise with which our children need help. We need to be approachable. One way to open the conversation door is to relate stories to our children from own our childhood. I did that with my children. I will never forget Julie Farmer from seventh grade. She was bigger than me and was my personal bully! One day at lunch, I got up from my seat beside my friends to get my food. When I returned, Julie had taken my seat and refused to get up. In those days many girls had *formed* hairdos, none of that hair blowing in the wind stuff. On that day, I had all I could take from Julie Farmer. I left the table, but returned behind Julie and poured my carton of chocolate milk on her head. Her formed hairdo was the perfect slide for that chocolate milk! I still chuckle thinking about it, until I think about how Julie Farmer must have felt. My children will never forget that story, but hopefully they were impacted by the lessons of what not to do in the same situation. In addition, they learned what happened when I lied to the principal about what I had done!

We need to really know our children and discern what is going on in their minds and lives. That becomes more difficult as they age. Talk to them every day, find some way to start a conversation. If you cannot get them to open up, tell them something silly you did, or even something sinful and how you handled it. Laughter is a great ice breaker. Our children need to know we are human and sinful just like them. My grown daughter and I have contact every day and I can still read between her lines.

Words that are truthful and spoken in love are not always easy to accept when sin is admonished. However, love does remove some of the sting and makes the words easy to come back to. The words we speak to our children will impact their lives for good or bad. What we are in life is factual, such as being a female, wife, and mother. Who we are in life changes with growth and is often impacted by what others say to us and think of us. The greatest impact comes from the words spoken by a parent. Words we speak to our children can mark them for life.

Remember the power of the tongue that we discussed in Chapter 1? A parent has more power in their speech with their children than they will ever understand. As a parent, we are our child's nurturer, provider, caregiver, and authority. When they are young, we are all that our children know and understand. Angry, abusive, mean, or selfish words are never spoken in love or for the best interest of our child. Telling children they are stupid, ugly, not worth anything, lazy (Need I go on?) will impact their entire lives. Our words need to be those of love, truth, encouragement, and building up. David told his Heavenly Father, *I have not departed from thy judgments: for thou hast taught me. How sweet are thy words unto my taste! Yea, sweeter than honey to my mouth!* (Psalm 119:102-103) God's words to

David were sweeter than honey. Let our words and communication with our children be pleasing before the Lord and edifying to them.

During the life of a child, parental conversations will deal with sinful behavior, habits that need to be addressed, handling of certain situations, while other conversations will just be informational. All through our lives there is a lot to learn—even the oldest adult still has things to learn. Remember, we do not know everything, and often situations are not always as they appear. Let us not be guilty of killing someone with accusations and asking questions later. None of us will reach perfection until we meet our Lord and Savior Jesus Christ. When we are quick to judge situations, we become unapproachable. We should never ridicule or mock anyone for something we think they should already know and understand, especially our children. We need to consider how important communication is in our lives. May the Lord help us to be good listeners, to be slow to speak, and to choose our words very carefully.

The Importance of Fathers

A father and mother each play an important role in the life of a daughter. A daughter's first impression and understanding of God and authority comes from her view of her father. A father is first seen as the authority in the home. God's chain of command is Himself, the husband (or father), and then the wife (or mother). This chain of command is confirmed in Ephesians 5:23: *For the husband is the head of the wife, even as Christ is the head of the church: and he is the Saviour of the body.* Women and children are under the umbrella of authority of the husband and father. That umbrella of authority does not make void a woman or child's personal responsibility to accept Christ as Savior or to personally account for their sin.

All through the Old Testament we find repeated stories of entire families that suffered blessing or judgment based on the actions and leading of the husband and father. The word *father* is found over

1500 times in Scripture, which includes references to our Heavenly Father. The word *mother* is only found 299 times. The fact that the Lord God set men as the authority over women does not devalue the worth of women. It means that God made men and women different, each having a role of great importance to God. It means that someone has to lead and be in charge; while others have to follow. *For Adam was first formed, then Eve.* (1 Timothy 2:13) This is God's order and we need to abide by it. It is essential that daughters learn God's chain of command at an early age. The importance of following the father's leadership becomes crucial during our daughter's teen years. As mothers, we set the tone in our home. Our actions and responses to our husband's authority will greatly influence our daughter's responses.

In addition to the leadership role, the father also plays another important part in the life of his daughter. That important part is approval and acceptance of his daughter. Just as a child of God seeks the approval and acceptance of the Heavenly father, a daughter needs the approval and acceptance of her earthly father. Approval and acceptance come as the father leads and trains his daughter and she follows. A daughter learns to follow from her mother. Leading and training by a father requires daily interaction. A young lady desperately needs interaction in her life with her father. A father's presence in the home and provision of needs is not enough. A girl first understands men, their role in life, their behavior, and how to interact with them through her father. If a strong relationship with her father is lacking in a daughter's life, she will have difficulty as she gets older and interacts with men in the world. Unfortunately, the world emphasizes and operates around physical attraction. If a young lady does not learn proper interaction between men and women at home, she will take her cue from the world. Worldly cues will lead her down the path of focusing on physical attraction.

Sometimes a father may not lead and interact with a daughter to the degree that he should. He may not understand the need, may not know how to interact on a deeper level, or may not have the desire. The most important way we as wives can address this issue is through prayer. The Apostle Paul told the people of Thessalonica that they prayed for them so *that our God would count you worthy of this calling, and fulfill all the good pleasure of his goodness, and the work of faith with power.* (2 Thessalonians 1:11b) What an awesome calling for a man to be a father. We ought to pray that our husband fulfills his calling as a father. Pray specifically that he will be the father he needs to be to his girls and boys.

We can also encourage our husbands to be better fathers. A good way to start is to accentuate the positive. Always build up his positive traits, characteristics, and actions. Tell him the things you love about him and/or write him personal notes. Statements like, *Lucy really enjoyed going to the park with you today* can really bolster their desire to do more. Encouraging words are like dessert after a meal. We all love dessert and would be motivated to do more to obtain it!

Recently the daughter of our pastor turned ten years old. To mark the event he took her on a short trip to New York. I already knew from observation that he spent quality time with all three of his children, but that trip really raised my admiration for him as a father. His daughter will never forget that trip, nor the time spent with her father. My son has three daughters that he frequently takes individually on daddy dates. Those are precious times that will do much to build the lives of his daughters.

Unfortunately, today there are Christian homes all over America without a father. A single mom cannot fill the role of a missing dad. An alternative for women in this situation is to find help in their home church. Keep the children in church. Spend time with other Christian families that have fathers. Ask for involvement with your children from a good spiritually strong young pastor and his wife. If there is a saved grandfather or uncle living close to the family, request their involvement with the children. Christian husbands and wives need to be alert to those in their church family in a single parent environment and help where they are able. All through the Scriptures, the fatherless and widows are addressed as those that we should care for. James tells us that *pure religion and undefiled before God and the Father is this, to visit the fatherless and widows in their affliction, and to keep himself unspotted from the world.* (James 1:27) Of course the best help for single parents will come from the Lord through prayer. He will always help. *When my father and my mother forsake me, then the Lord will take me up.* (Psalm 27:10)

Homes where the father is absent can be a lot like homes where the father does not know the Lord as his Savior. Unsaved husbands often live for self and the family is not the priority it should be. Although, there are many unsaved husbands who are very moral upright men, who often function better than a saved husband. They provide for their families and have a very integral part in the lives of their families. The key components that are missing in a home with an unsaved father are having God at the center and the family being led in the path that God would have. No one can really begin to properly fulfill their role in this life without knowing Jesus as their Savior. Properly means God's way. Scripture is very clear that wives are to submit to their husbands (Ephesians 5:22). I noticed long ago that the Scriptures never tells us to submit to our husbands **if they are saved.** We are to honor and submit to our husbands whether they are saved or not. In like manner, we should be sure our children do the same. No matter the situation or atmosphere in our homes, we should always love, honor, and respect our husbands. We will talk more about unsaved husbands in Chapter Four.

Friends

The ultimate perfect friend for every Christian is the Lord Jesus Christ. Our best human friends are those who follow Christ. Those we spend time with will have a tremendous impact in our lives. *Make no friendship with an angry man; and with a furious man*

thou shalt not go: lest thou learn his ways, and get a snare to thy soul.
(Proverbs 22:24-25) Our children's friends and acquaintances will
greatly influence them. We need to supervise this aspect of their
lives as late into their teen years as possible. Peer pressure has to be
the number one area of concern for teens and parents. It is much
easier to commit sin we would not normally commit, when we are
with others. Peer pressure is a lifelong issue for all of us; however,
the teen years suffer the greatest impact. *My son, if sinners entice
thee, consent thou not.* (Proverbs 1:10) Sinners will entice our teens
and the world will draw them, because our children are sinners.
I mentioned earlier that the teen years are a time when our teen
looks outside of her family and into the world. She will want to
identify with those who will accept her; especially if she feels a lack
of acceptance at home. Acceptance is a key issue for a teen.

As a child emerges from childhood, their character and personality
really begin to blossom. Often we as parents want our daughters
to be more like us or even just different from who they are. Every
child is different and has qualities gifted from God. Think of it
this way—God has crafted a unique, priceless vessel and gifted us
with that vessel. A child is a precious gift from God. We need to
celebrate the uniqueness of each child and mold that uniqueness
into what God has for them. Some parents need to take the first
step of accepting their children for who they are. Scripture tells us
that *children are an heritage from the Lord: and the fruit of the womb
is his reward.* (Psalm 127:3) Children are a heritage and a reward from
God. Many parents have forgotten this truth. We need to accept
our children for who they are or they will seek that acceptance in
other places and from other people.

My children were fortunate to attend Christian school for a major
part of their education. I was a working mom, so home schooling
was not an option for us. The choice of schooling is a matter
that a husband and wife have to settle with the Lord, to do as
He leads. I was thrilled when the Lord placed in my husband the
desire for our children to start at a Christian school as our son

entered seventh grade and our daughter fourth grade. A Christian school environment would place them in a protected Christian environment—or so I thought. Please do not misunderstand me, the school was excellent. However, it did not take me long to learn that all who attend a Christian school are not necessarily saved or walking closely with the Lord. The unsaved world sees a lot of benefit in sending their children to a Christian school because of the good environment. That being said, my children's friends at school were not always the influence that I would have chosen for them.

My daughter's friends were nice and seemingly well-behaved. One friend was the sort that I knew would encourage her spiritually and would promote good clean fun. Another friend gave me great concern. Unfortunately, my daughter was drawn to this young lady and we always butted heads over their association. My daughter felt that I just did not like the girl and I found no words that could convince her that the problem was something altogether different. God gives mothers a special intuition for a reason. I knew in my heart that this particular friend was not going in the same direction I wanted for my daughter. Recently, my daughter ran into this friend. She came back, now at age 32, and told me that I was right in trying to dissuade her from being with this friend. In addition, she told me of some of the things that they did during sleepovers at the friend's home, which were not good. This young lady and her parents were decent people in the world, just not living their lives aligned with the Lord. Looking back, I realize I should have made better choices for that situation, regardless of whether my daughter understood or not. *Chasten thy son while there is hope, and let not thy soul spare for his crying.* (Proverbs 19:18) I still to this day spare the crying child to their detriment! If I could give two tips to parents of teenagers it would be: pray for the Lord to send your children good friends all through their life and do not ignore the intuition He gives you. We do the very best we can as parents with the Lord's help and we leave the rest to Him.

As mothers we need to be very involved with our daughters and their friends. I made it a point to also be with the mothers of the friends. I planned as many activities as possible at our home or with me present. I planned activities to include those I wanted my daughter to spend time with. Also, I planned activities so mothers and daughters could be together. We went shopping, out to lunch, and even on day trips to nearby cities. Keeping daughters busy with activities gives them less time to be with friends we would rather they avoid. I have known quite a few Christian families (especially homeschoolers) that limit their children's interaction with other children outside of church activities with good results. I tried to go to as many school functions as possible, so that I could be around my daughter and her friends. The school our children attended was 26 miles from our home and their friends were spread out over a large area. I made the effort to go the distance to be with my children and to see they were with good friends. It was well worth it.

Recently in our community an 11 year old girl died by hanging herself. She attended a church school where she was being bullied about her weight. This story is horribly repeated all over this country on a regular basis. Spending much time with our children and their friends will hopefully give us a sense of what is really going on in their lives. When our son was young, for a time he was having constant stomach aches and did not want to go to school. I knew something was up. In talking with him, we finally learned that an older boy was threatening him in the bathroom at school. He was told he would be killed if he told anyone. We thank the Lord that He helped us take care of the problem and there were no repercussions for our son.

When my son was young, children generally did not have to deal with bullying when they were not in school. However, that is not the case today. Email, social media, game stations, and cell phones permit bullying to continue well past the school environment. Constant monitoring of our children's computer and other devices are vitally important. Log into social media from your child's device, this will enable you to see the comments and posts directed at them. Staying in tune with our children and their friends is an essential practice that will help us get our children through the teen years.

Femininity

I remember seeing an interview once of an actor who played the father in a wholesome family television show from the 70s. During the interview, he was asked about his real life wife. As the gentlemen described his wife, he described femininity in a way that I have not forgotten. He was most attracted to his wife when she was getting ready for her day: the delicate lace of the under garments, the sweet smells, and her womanhood. Femininity is that which is characteristic of a woman. The actor's comments also reminded me that God created men to be attracted and drawn to women by sight. Sweet smells certainly help as well.

Do you remember the story of Esther? The women that were candidates to be the new queen made great preparation before they went in before the king. They took twelve months to prepare their bodies. *According to the manner of women, (for so were the days of their purification accomplished, to wit, six months with oil of myrrh, and six months with sweet odours, and with other things for the purifying of the women;).* (Esther 2:12b) Delicacy, softness, gentleness, and sweet smells are the outward indicators of femininity. Unfortunately, those attributes are diminished in today's society. We have given much over to our comfort and to conformity. T-shirts, sweats, pajama pants, and jeans are widespread. Dressing like the world is common for today's Christian. Ribbons, lace, bows, curls, and sweet smells still rein in little girlhood, but not so much after that. The world's way of dress often unifies (as in unisex) men and women.

Gender specific clothing is blurred today. Have you ever been in the ladies room at Wal-Mart and had this sudden fear come over you when you noticed the clothing parts of the person in the next stall? Did you wonder if you had accidently walked into the wrong restroom? I have on more than one occasion. I wonder if I have ever horrified someone in the next stall. Sometimes I ask myself if someone saw me from the back, neck down, would they wonder if I were male or female by my clothing. Today hair length is not always an indicator. It certainly is not necessary for women to wear bustles, corset's, and hoop dresses. Although I could easily have lived in an era with that type of woman's dress, as opposed to today.

We as Christian women need to make certain there is never a doubt as to which gender we are or which gender we identify with. *The woman shall not wear that which pertaineth unto a man, neither shall a man put on a woman's garment: for all that do so are abomination unto the Lord thy God.* (Deuteronomy 22:5) That which pertains to a man is that which society prepares and sells as men's clothing or that which society would associate with a man. Today differentiating between men and women's clothing is sometimes difficult. A sweatshirt or t-shirt and jeans in both the men's and women's department look exactly the same. I have noticed one helpful distinction with clothing. Buttons on a man's shirt are on the right side of the shirt and a woman's are on the left. The flap that covers the zipper on men's pants is on the left and women's is on the right. Interestingly, I found that the flap on both men and women's jeans are on the left. Ladies, please don't misunderstand, I am not speaking against wearing jeans. I am trying to point out that women are losing their feminine distinctiveness.

Often Christians, in an effort to fit in or be comfortable, accidently identify themselves with the opposite sex. Paul tells us in Romans that Christians should not be *conformed to this world: but be transformed by the renewing of your mind, that ye may prove what is that good, and acceptable, and perfect, will of God.* (Romans 12:2) One way we conform to the world is by dressing like the world.

Clothing is just another area where society attempts to contradict the differences that God placed in men and women.

Clothing can be a huge hurdle for our teenage daughters. There is so much pressure from the world for a teenager to fit in. Modest and appropriate clothing choices are very limited today. God's Word has many passages, which we will explore, that can be used to set clothing standards in our homes. As with anything in our homes, fathers and mothers need to come together and agree ahead of time in this matter of dress. Setting a dress standard ahead of time leaves less room for issues with our children. Young ladies need to know why there are dress standards in our home. It is important to teach them how our dress should be pleasing to the Lord, whom we represent as Christians.

It is also important for our daughters to understand that young men can be sexually aroused when they are inappropriately dressed. This explains why modesty is the most important issue with a young lady and her clothing. *In like manner also, that women adorn themselves in modest apparel.* (1 Timothy 2:9a) The word modest means *orderly or good behavior*, which is simple to understand. However, to properly understand and apply the verse we need to understand what *like manner* is referring to. Paul explains in verse 8, *I will therefore that men pray everywhere, lifting up holy hands, without wrath and doubting.* (1 Timothy 2:8)

A woman's modest dress should be like men who can pray anywhere and are always ready to come before the Lord. Modest dress is like holy hands, always concentrated and clean (or pure) before the Lord. Modest dress is also without wrath and doubting. One meaning for the word wrath in I Timothy 2:8 is *indignation or anger* because something is not fair. Modest dress should be without indignation. This is an interesting statement to me. Paul is teaching Timothy, as a young preacher, in this passage. It is easy to understand why modesty could have been an issue for Timothy to address given the nature of the Greek culture. Judging by their immodest statutes, there must have been an issue with inappropriately dressed ladies. Paul was always very practical to address specific issues. I wonder if Christian ladies during that time thought it unfair not to be able to dress like the culture. Does that sound like a familiar thought concerning teenage girls?

I also found the word doubting very interesting as well. That word means *disputing or with discussion*. Modest dress should be without disputing or discussion. What could be disputed? The answer would be Biblical guidelines. It is studies like these that truly reveal that the Bible is timeless and always appropriate! In today's language the clothing of a young lady or a woman should be orderly, concentrated in faith, pure, without dispute or discussion. You may ask if orderly dress means neat and in orderly array. Yes, that is certainly included, but let us takes this one step further; orderly dress does not cause disorder.

When a female wears clothes that are revealing it will cause disorder. A long time ago, in a Wednesday night church service a lady visitor came in after the preaching had begun. She was nicely dressed with a lovely fur wrap about her shoulders. After she had been seated for a short time, she decided to remove her wrap. The service became disorderly as people moved in their seats and attention drew to that lady. She was wearing a dress that stopped above her breast line and under her arms; it had no shoulders or neckline. We may think, "Oh is that all," because that is the world's attitude today. However, it was enough to cause disorder. Every time a woman dresses immodestly, no matter her age, there is disorder in some form or manner. She calls inappropriate attention to herself and provokes men to look at her. A group of young men can be engaged in any activity, such as playing a sport or fixing a car, and when an immodestly dressed young lady appears on the scene, there will be disorder. If Christian parents could read the thoughts of teenage boys as they gawk at their immodestly dressed daughters, there would never be a dress issue.

The more skin we show, the more loudly we proclaim that we are not ashamed of displaying our body. We may also be proclaiming something we would rather not. Nakedness in the Scriptures is most often associated with sexual relations. Leviticus chapter 20 forbids uncovering the nakedness of those we are not to have sexual relations with. Unfortunately, women who uncover their nakedness are often associated with women with loose morals, who participate in sexual sin. In Genesis 38, Judah committed sin with his own daughter-in-law, because she disguised herself and wore the clothes of a harlot. Lack of modesty in worldly clothing today leaves many Christians thinking it is okay to dress the same to fit in.

Christian ladies, our bodies belong to the Lord and should be consecrated before Him. Nakedness in the Bible is also related to shame. *Behold, I come as a thief. Blessed is he that watcheth, and keepeth his garments, lest he walk naked, and they see his shame.* (Revelation 16:15) Young ladies need to be taught exactly what nakedness is, so there will be no confusion as to why they should not dress like the world. Low cleavage, exposed mid-drift, revealed thighs, and see-through clothing are not the only forms of nakedness today. There is also something I call nakedness in high definition color. I am not talking about what can be found on the television. Nakedness in high definition color is when the clothing worn is so tight that the body outline is just as visible as it would be without the clothes. A good example is leggings. I love leggings under my skirts and dresses in the winter time; they add extra warmth. Unfortunately, the latest trend for many women is to turn leggings into pants. When I see women wearing exposed leggings, I am ashamed for them. I wonder if they realize they are walking around naked with just a colored layered skin on top. The outline of the body with every bump and every bulge is exposed. The same applies to tight fitting pants and clingy dresses which show a woman's body.

Ladies, our clothing or lack of it identifies us, defines who we are, our attitudes, and our convictions. Often we are prejudged by our clothing. Girls and young ladies learn how to dress from their mothers. Unsaved ladies will never change their clothing preferences until they get saved. Christian ladies need to grow spiritually and learn what the Lord wants in this area of clothing. We need to be gentle with immature Christians in this area of dress. However, an attitude that says, "I will wear what I want" or "I have a beautiful body, I will show it off" is a sinful attitude that needs to be dealt with. As Christian parents, we need to be ever vigilant in this matter of our daughter's clothing.

Today's fashion and styles draw our girls' attention. We need to be creative and find ways for them to be fashionable, but modest. We don't want to fit into the world, but we do not want to stick out like a sore thumb either. Getting our daughters involved with finding alternative appropriate clothing helps them feel they are involved in the choices. My daughter-in-law suggested fashion designing materials for our granddaughters' Christmas gifts. Fashion designing is an awesome way for them to work on appropriate clothing choices. Another suggestion is layered clothing for all seasons, which is fashionable today. A mid-drift revealing top can be worn over a solid colored t-shirt. A low-cut shirt works with a t-shirt underneath. Looking stylish in appropriate clothing can be a task. The majority of the world is against us on this issue. However, one person with God is a greater majority. It is God's desire that we dress appropriately and He will help us, if we ask!

Dating

One thing is very evident from Scripture in this matter of girl and boy relationships before marriage—the strong involvement of parents. Most marriage ceremony vows include the words, *Therefore shall a man leave his father and his mother, and shall cleave unto his wife: and they shall be one flesh.* (Genesis 2:24) It is obvious that this verse means the husband and wife leave the parents behind and cleave to each other. However, the other side that is evident is that they leave a tight bond or relationship with the parents. The word leave in Genesis 2:24 means *to loosen.* I believe that God intends for children to have a strong relationship with their parents.

In the time frame that the Bible was written, Christian marriages were arranged by the parent of the young man. Arranged marriage did not mean that the young man had no say in the matter; we recall that Samson asked his parents for a certain young lady. (Judges 14:1-2) Today the pre-marital process is quite different in the world. Young men and woman search (most often on their own) and find their intended mate with little input from parents. Often, couples date before the parents have met the dating partner. Parents should be an important part of a child's dating process. Parents have a God-given intuition and experience that are vital to a child making a good judgment in finding a mate.

Regrettably today, many young couples choose to live together before marriage. It appears the thought process is to **try things out** before making a permanent commitment. Jason Koebler reported in the April 4, 2013 issue of *Newsweek* that the National Center for Health Statistics says that 48% of women *between 15 and 44 lived with a partner before getting married between the years of 2006 and 2010.* Even though our country is ever changing and progressing to a totally godless society, we must always remember God's Word never changes. The Scripture is very clear that sex before marriage or sex outside of marriage is sin. *Flee fornication. Every sin that a man doeth is without the body; but he that committeth fornication sinneth against his own body.* (1 Corinthians 6:18) *Now the works of the flesh are manifest, which are these; Adultery, fornication, uncleanness, lasciviousness.* (Galatians 5:19) *They which do* (practice) *such things shall not inherit the kingdom of God.* (Galatians 5:21b) God's people never enjoy God's blessings while walking contrary to His Word. We should always follow God's Word and not society's practice.

So what is the practice for Christian young people and their parents in this matter of dating and marriage? Christians should follow

God's process in finding a mate—that process in every Christian's life **always** starts with His Word and prayer.

Ask, and it shall be given you; seek, and ye shall find; knock, and it shall be opened unto you: For every one that asketh receiveth; and he that seeketh findeth; and to him that knocketh it shall be opened. (Matthew 7:7-8)

I know in my own life, any time I truly want to know the Lord's direction, He **always** reveals it. If we want to know God's will in this matter of marriage, God will reveal it. We need to remember that dating leads to marriage and marriage is a life changing decision that will impact the rest of our lives. It is so important to find God's choice for us. The first thing we know is that saved people should not be joined to unsaved people. Parents should establish this truth with their young people before they are of dating age.

Be ye not unequally yoked together with unbelievers: for what fellowship hath righteousness with unrighteousness? And what communion hath light with darkness? And what concord hath Christ with Belial? Or what part hath he that believeth with an infidel? (2 Corinthians 6:14-15)

Unfortunately, this is where some go astray. A young man or lady meets a nice, decent person of the opposite sex and they are drawn together. One party is not saved, but the other party feels there is a possibility the unsaved will come to know the Lord. The unsaved person is even willing to go to church. This type of situation is a dangerous one. Based on the verses above, God does not condone evangelistic dating or dating with the hopes of evangelizing the unsaved participant. This is the time in which parents need to prevent the relationship from going any further. Saved people should only be seeking a mate among other saved people. God was specific with the people of Israel from the very beginning. His instruction was to find a mate among their own people. We see this as Abraham sought a wife for Isaac.

And I will make thee (Abraham's servant) *swear by the Lord, the God of heaven, and the God of the earth, that thou shalt not take a wife*

unto my son of the daughters of the Canaanites, among whom I dwell:
But thou shalt go unto my country, and to my kindred, and take a wife
unto my son Isaac. (Genesis 24:3-4)

We see why this is so important in later passages. In Exodus 34:14-
16 God explains that Israel is to worship only Him. When the
Israelites took mates from among people who followed other gods,
they eventually turned them from the one true God. The same holds
true today. A saved person and an unsaved person are not going
in the same direction. Joining to an unsaved person in marriage
will pull the saved person away from the Lord and will cause great
difficulty in the marriage. King Solomon is a good example of
what occurs when we take a mate from among the unsaved. *But*
King Solomon loved many strange women. (1 Kings 11:1) We see that
Solomon's problem was twofold; he took multiple mates and took
them from among the heathen.

And he had seven hundred wives, princesses, and three hundred
concubines: and his wives turned away his heart. For it came to pass,
when Solomon was old, that his wives turned away his heart after
other gods: and his heart was not perfect with the Lord his God, as was
the heart of David his father. (1 Kings 11:3-4)

I wonder how it would feel as a Christian to come to the end of
our life and know we did not please God. The Christian's purpose
should always be to move closer to God and press toward that mark
of the high calling of God. An unsaved mate can impact a believer's
walk. The Lord God used King Solomon in a tremendous way in
the early years of his life; however, he did not finish strong for the
Lord. The primary reason for this is his choice to join with unsaved
women. As Christians, our people are other Christian people and
that is where we should find our life long marriage partner.

We also notice in Scripture the times when God brought the mate
to the marriage. A classic example of this is Adam and Eve. *And*
the rib, which the Lord God had taken from man, made he a woman,
and brought her unto the man. (Genesis 2:22) In addition, we see

that Abraham's servant, led by the Lord, brought Rebecca to Isaac (Genesis 24:66-67) and the Lord brought Ruth to Boaz (Ruth 3:10). The Lord does all things well and when He brings the mate we can never go wrong.

My son attended a small Christian school, with a limited amount of dating choices. When he graduated he attended a much larger Christian college. During his first year he was like a kid in a candy store. Every week he would tell me of a wonderful Christian young lady with whom he ate lunch or dinner. I was excited to see who the Lord would choose for him, although I was a little distraught at the possibility my son was doing the choosing and not the Lord. I remember speaking with him after one particular date with a young lady that he described as *just like me*. Later, when I asked how she was, his response was, "Who?" He had moved on to the next young lady after only a week.

As the end of his freshman year came to a close, some of his Christian friends decided they better talk to him. I am so glad they did. His friends told him his testimony was being marred by his *variety* dating. He took the admonishment to heart and decided to pray and let the Lord bring the right mate to him. And of course He did. A young lady he met at the end of his freshman year came back into his life soon after the start of the sophomore year. I have to say the Lord brought him the perfect godly wife, because I can find no fault in her! *The Lord is good unto them that wait for him, to the soul that seeketh him.* (Lamentations 3:25)

Often it takes time for God's choice in a mate to come along. Don't fret; the wait is worth it! I can remember praying from the time my children were young for their future mates. Some may ask, "Why pray?" It is God's will to put Christian people together in marriage. This is true; however, we pray for our children to seek and do God's will. Praying to the Lord always needs to be specific. When we pray for our children and their future mates we can pray for the following: the Lord to prepare our child for their intended mate; that both would be saved at a young age; that both would be students of God's Word; that they are faithful people in the place the Lord calls them to; that our daughter's husband would be a hard worker and good provider; etc.

There are so many areas to pray for regarding our children. Once our children are saved, they may step off the path God has laid out for their lives. We may not prevent a step off the path, but we have a responsibility to do everything we can to keep them on the path the Lord has for them. Just like the shepherd prods the little sheep along the path he has for them, we prod our children. We should always be moving them on God's path and towards Him and His will for their lives. Amen!

College

God has a purpose and specific plan for every human life He creates. The plan for the unsaved is for them to first know Him as their Savior. The foremost plan for a Christian is to witness to others about the Lord, to walk with Him daily, and follow His Word. *The steps of a good man are ordered by the Lord: and he delighteth in his way.* (Psalms 37:23) Young people need guidance from the Word of God and their parents to know God's will for their lives. In many instances, God's will is plainly revealed in His Word; in other situations, specific leading from God has to reveal His will. Education is an important necessity in all lives. Education in God's Word is the most important; however, secular education has its place as well. Decisions about higher education are between the parent and the child as they discern what God has for the child. It seems the norm among Christians today is for a young man to attend college to further his education in whatever God has called Him to do. However, it is not always as apparent for a young lady as to whether she should attend college. In fact, I remember thinking about that before my daughter attended college. She did not really have a desire to go, but she did. During college, my daughter was very homesick and wanted to come home the entire time. I always questioned whether her father and I did the right thing by pushing her to go. It would not be until much later that I would learn that answer through situations in my own life.

While our daughter attended college, she often remarked about the type of degree most young ladies were seeking. That degree was the MRS degree. Since I had not attended college before that time, I actually thought there was a real MRS degree. Much to my surprise, the MRS degree referred to young ladies attending college to find a husband. It is true that many find their mate in college, but finding a mate should not be the reason to attend. College tuition is a huge price to pay to find a mate, but many have paid that price! We understand that God created men and women for marriage and multiplying. If a young lady is destined to marriage and caring for a home and a child, is college important? The answer is *yes* and I will explain why.

According to Wikipedia, the average life expectancy for a woman in the United States is 82.2 years. That is a long span of time in which a woman has many roles to fill. Once I decided to write out on note cards all of the jobs I had to do. I showed my husband—he was not impressed! However, it prepared me to tell you. Some of the tasks we as women may be called on to do in our lifetime include handling finances for our home and possibly our parents or grandparents; household management and scheduling; nutrition planning; health diagnosis and management; event planning and coordination; teaching; counseling; and the list goes on. College may not teach us all we need to be a good wife and mother, but it certainly will expose us to many things that will aid us during our lifetime.

There will come a point in our lives when our children are grown. We may need to work or even help our husband in a ministry. In today's society, some women work all through married life. We need to be prepared to do the best we can at whatever we are called to do in this life. *Study to shew thyself approved unto God, a workman that needeth not to be ashamed, rightly dividing the word of truth.* (2 Timothy 2:15) I know this verse is generally applied to studying God's Word. Nevertheless, in order to be a good *workwoman*, we often need education in certain areas. We are to glorify the Lord in all areas of our lives. Being educationally prepared will help us do our very best. The possibilities of what the Lord may call us to do are endless. The Lord sees the entire path we are on—we only see the past and present. The Lord is always preparing us today for something He has for us tomorrow.

In September 2012, at the age of 54, I received my college diploma. I was married at 18 and a bookkeeper at age 19. I did not have the opportunity to attend college when I was young, but always wanted to. After our children completed college, I felt the Lord leading me to obtain my CPA licensing. My husband agreed, so I embarked on a six year college journey. As I took college accounting courses, I saw how unnecessarily complex our government has made our tax laws. The desire to become a CPA faded over time. I told my husband I was not sure what the Lord would have me do, but I knew He would reveal it at some point—and, of course, He did.

In the summer of 2013, the Lord amazingly birthed in my heart a desire to write to teach other Christian women. In elementary and high school, my grammar and English skills were very poor. However, an amazing thing happened during college. My writing skills greatly improved after writing many, many papers. It became obvious that the Lord was preparing me for a different path. My grammar and English skills are still lacking, but the Lord has blessed me with many friends who willingly give their time to proofread my writing. In December 2013, my first book was published— *Dear Sister in Christ.* You are reading my second book now. What we are doing today may seem insignificant or unimportant, but the Lord uses everything in our lives. *And we know that all things work together for good to them that love God, to them who are called according to his purpose.* (Romans 8:28)

Some women may never have the opportunity to attend college; they still do their best for the Lord with the skills they have. The Lord can always use a life yielded to Him. Each young lady, with the Lord and her parents, has to decide what is right for her life and her path with the Lord. Education makes no one better than the other. College just lends a little more information and practice to strengthen our God-given abilities. Remember the Lord expects excellence from us in whatever we do in this life. *Whether therefore you eat, or drink, or whatsoever ye do, do all to the glory of God.* (1 Corinthians 10:31)

Conclusion

There are many areas to deal with in the life of our teenage daughters. We have discussed the most important issues. Obviously, communication is at the top of the list. Communication with the Lord, between husband and wife, and between parent and child is the first hurdle to conquering teenage difficulties. Fathers have such an influence in their homes and with their daughters. Their involvement, or lack thereof, plays such an important part in the transition of a young lady. We should pray for our husbands daily as they lead our homes and families. Exercising godly wisdom and judgment in the matter of our daughter's friends, clothing, dating, and college decisions is imperative. *Watch ye and pray, lest ye enter into temptation.* (Mark 14:38a) The word *watch* in this verse means to *be sleepless and vigilant.* There is no time in the life of our child more than the teenage years that we need to be vigilant. We need to do our very best and leave the rest to our Lord. Amen!

Chapter 2 Review

1. What do you feel is the number one issue that Christian teens have to deal with?

2. For the issue you listed in question 1, can you find a verse that would help a parent address that issue? List the verse reference.

3. As a child goes into the teens years, at what age can we leave them to their selves? Read Proverbs 29:15. What does the verse mean when it says *left to himself*?

4. One main area of conflict between a teen and their parent can be communication. Do you agree? Why do you agree or disagree?

5. Read Proverbs 25:11. What does the word *fitly* mean?

6. Do you think that communication with parent and child is similar to our communication with the Lord? If so, how?

7. Read Proverbs 1:10. Is enticement the same as peer pressure?

8. Do you think it is easier to sin if you have a partner in crime?

9. Name one possible result of having unsaved friends. (See James 4:4)

10. Read Deuteronomy 22:5 and look up the words. What do you think this verse means?

11. Look up the word *modest* and write the definition.

12. Read 1 John 2:15-16 and write one way we can teach this to a teen.

13. What is the main role of the father in a home? Read Ephesians 5:22-6:4

14. For a woman that is a single parent, what suggestion would you make to help her fill the gap of the missing father figure in her home?

15. How important is a father in the life of a daughter? Answer from your own experience.

16. Find a verse that God gives that warns us not to marry an unsaved person.

17. What is evangelistic dating?

18. How many dates should a Christian girl attend before she breaks off the relationship with a person she knows is not her lifelong mate?

Chapter 3

The Most Important Trait: Faith

The topic of faith is my favorite, because it is crucial to our Christian life. We are saved by faith; we live by faith; and we overcome the world by faith. Faith indeed is the victory! One of my favorite Bible verses is: *but without faith it is impossible to please him:* (Hebrews 11:6a) I surely want to please God in my life and I am sure you do as well. I want to please the Lord because I love Him, but I often feel I do not love Him enough. My desire is to love Him more. We can never love the Lord enough, especially when we compare our love to His love. What does love have to do with faith? Love has a lot to do with faith. Actually, the two are teammates and we cannot have one without the other. *Faith which worketh by love.* (Galatians 5:6b)

The object of a Christian's faith is the Lord God. Faith gives hope and hope produces a great love for God and who He is. On the other side of the coin, the more we know God, the more we love Him; the more we love Him, the more we trust him. The stories in Scripture of the saints and their faith in God teach us what faith looks like and the results of having faith. Preacher Adrian Rogers says that faith *is not getting from God what we want; it is receiving from God what He gives.* What a statement. We all want to receive what we desire and what we think is best for us. Real faith trusts God to give us what He thinks we need. If we really know Him and love Him, we can have great faith!

What is Faith?

The simple definition of faith is *believing and trusting*. A person can believe without trusting, but they cannot trust without believing. So faith can only exist by believing and trusting. Often faith is seen as a system of beliefs, such as the Baptist faith. The *Encarta Dictionary* defines faith as *belief in, devotion to, or trust in somebody or something, especially without logical proof.* The phrase, *without logical proof,* makes me smile. I am glad I have an awesome God in my life whose actions and leadings are not logical! Christian faith rests upon a God that cannot be seen, which may seem irrational to an unsaved world. If we could rationalize who God really is and how He works, we would not have to exercise faith.

Let's look at how the Scriptures define faith. *Now faith is the substance of things hoped for, the evidence of things not seen.* (Hebrews 11:1) The word substance in this verse means *assurance, or confidence.* So then faith is made up of, or its substance is, assurance and confidence. Assurance and confidence, which is placed in God and His Word.

Many people have faith in a lot of other things today besides God, such as leaders, wealth, and themselves. Faith that is not placed in God will fail. Christians who continually fail to trust the Lord will doubt their salvation. We must have full assurance and confidence in His Word. Everything we know about God comes from His Word. Not only are the Scriptures the only source of knowledge of God, they also are the power of God. *For I am not ashamed of the gospel of Christ: for it is the power of God unto salvation to everyone that believeth.* (Romans 1:16a) It is by the power of God's Word that we are drawn to salvation. It is by the power of God's Word that He convicts us of sin and how we ought to live.

Unfortunately, in today's world there is a lot of controversy over God's Word. This is nothing new. There was a lot of controversy over God's Word even in the Apostle Paul's day, which he addressed in his writings. The controversy is caused by false teaching. God's Word is often questioned. Preachers and teachers today are regularly taking the Word of God out of context. Christians under false preaching and teaching will have an unstable faith and may even question their faith in God. When God's Word is mishandled or taken out of context, there appears to be a contradiction in His Word. A contradiction means there is a difference in two ideas that makes either idea seem impossible to be true. Any teaching that renders God's Word false is false teaching. If God's Word is not true in all parts, then none of it can be trusted. King David said of God's Word, *thy Word is true from the beginning: and every one of thy righteous judgments endureth forever.* (Psalm 119:160) All 176 verses of Psalm 119 speak about God's Word. When God's Word is taken out of context, it is taken to mean something it was not intended to mean. Many Christian's are confused and living defeated lives today, because they are following false teaching and misused Scriptures.

We Christians need to study the Word of God for ourselves, instead of allowing others to provide our complete information. God's Word is so important and precious. In the Word, we find Him! *In the beginning was the Word, and the Word was with God, and the Word was God.* (John 1:1) We need to know the Lord personally beyond His Word. We do that through His Word, but the focus is on Him and not just gaining knowledge. We need to read and study the Word looking for Him.

A few years ago I did a study on the character of God. I had a study sheet that someone else had created. Each day a different characteristic of God was studied, such as: He is our rock, He is merciful, He gives peace, etc. There were over fifty characteristics of God in the study. The study really opened my eyes to what an awesome God we have and serve. Our desire should be like the Apostle Paul's: *that I may know him, and the power of his resurrection, and the fellowship of his sufferings, being made conformable unto his death.* (Philippians 3:10) The term *to know* in the Scripture usually refers to knowing on a very deep level. What does knowing Him have to do with faith? I am glad you asked. The more we know The

Lord, who He is, and His character, the more we know He can be trusted.

The next part of the definition of faith found in Hebrews 11:1 says, that faith is *the substance of things hoped for*. What things are *hoped for*? Every time we exercise faith, we are hoping to gain something or for something to happen. When I ask my husband for money to go shopping, I hope he will grant my request based on his ability to comply. Hope is founded in the belief that something is possible. We hope something is possible, when we can see the ability exists for it to happen. If we cannot see or believe that there is a possibility, we have no hope.

When we know and understand the Lord, we know all things are possible with Him. Hope in the Lord plus faith in Him takes this one step further to expecting and anticipating. Donald Trump has the ability to give me one million dollars. I can hope that he would do so; but I would not have any reason to expect he would give the money, even though he is able to do so. However, if he sends me a letter stating that I have found his favor and a check would be coming for one million dollars, I would expect and anticipate the check to come based on his word and his ability. The God of all creation has sent us His Word with many, many promises to us. *Now unto him that is able to do exceeding abundantly above all that we ask or think.* (Ephesians 3:20a) *But my God shall supply all your need according to his riches in glory by Christ Jesus.* (Philippians 4:19) *When the wicked, even mine enemies and my foes, came upon me to eat up my flesh, they stumbled and fell.* (Psalm 27:2) We are children of the Heavenly King, yet we live as spiritual paupers every day!

I often wonder why we, as Christians, cannot take God at His Word and expect what He has for us. I am then reminded of what happens in my own life. In my mind I know so many of God's promises, but often Satan whispers, "but will He do it for you?" The only situation that prevents God's promises and blessings in our lives is when we have known sin that we refuse to confess and forsake. If we are walking with the Lord and are clean from sin, we should expect His promises to have full effect in our lives.

In the fall of 1998, my daughter and I were with her friend and the friend's mother on a shopping trip at the Myrtle Beach outlets. We began discussing how God could provide a mate. The girls were excited about their junior year in high school and attending the junior-senior event. However, they were distraught over the fact that there did not seem to be any date candidates for them at school or at church. Of course, the friend's mother and I were trying to encourage the girls to have faith in the Lord. We stressed that God could do anything. In my zealousness I said, "God could make a guy fall out of the sky if He wanted to." Boy, did I give the Lord something to laugh about that day! It made the girls laugh too, which was good because they had been in tears about the matter.

Several weeks later, I was getting groceries and a strange thing happened in the frozen food department at the store. No, a guy did not fall from the sky, but almost! A gentleman approached me and asked if I knew of a good independent Baptist church in the area. Of course, I am always ready to tell anyone about church! The gentlemen and his family were from Indiana visiting. I told him where I went and gave him the directions and service times. As we were talking, I saw a lady look out from around the frozen food cooler; then, the heads of four children popped out behind her! It was the man's family; they had six children in all. Of course you will never guess, but among the children was a young man my daughter's age! He was exactly her type: tall, dark, handsome, and a Christian! I could hear in my head, *blue light special on aisle nine!* I got to meet the family and was told I would see them in church the next day. They would be in Charleston for a week. I was so excited I could barely get out of the grocery store and get home. My poor daughter thought something horrific had happened as I rushed in the door to tell her the story! We both literally jumped up and down, as if Donald Trump had sent that check!

That dear family was faithful to church every service while on their vacation. In addition, the whole family sang together and blessed our church with wonderful singing. My daughter spent time with that young man and his sister on several occasions during that week. Although he would not be her date for the prom or even her permanent life mate, the Lord taught us a very valuable lesson that week. It was a lesson we would need later as she waited for her life's mate. The Barnes family continued to visit Charleston and we all have remained good friends over the years. God can and will provide exactly what we need for this life, and not always in what we can see. My daughter married at age 28 and yes, the Lord brought her another tall, dark, handsome Christian! He is her perfect mate. Thank You, Lord, for loving us so much!

The final part of our definition on faith states that faith is *the evidence of things not seen*. What is not seen? The only reasonable answer is God. *No man hath seen God at any time.* (John 1:18a) Faith and trust in God is something that can only be understood by the person that has it and applies it. However, the evidence of it can be seen by everyone around them. Evidence is proof of something. A good example of the evidence that I exist is my human form. Evidence is what is used in a court of law to prove a case or a point.

I really struggled with this part of the verse and wanted to understand it completely. My question was: Is the evidence or proof for us or for others? I came to the conclusion, it is for both. We have to remember our sentence parts again; *the evidence of things not seen* refers back to faith. Our faith in God is proof that He exists, not that He needs us in any way to prove His existence. When we exercise faith in God and in His Word, we see the results. Those results prove to us He is who He says He is and He does what He says He will do. Not only does that bear proof for us, it is proof for others. God says in Malachi 3:10:

Bring ye all the tithes into the storehouse, that there may be meat in mine house, and prove me now herewith, saith the Lord of hosts, if I will not open you the windows of heaven, and pour you out a blessing, that there shall not be room enough to receive it.

The God of Heaven tells us in this verse to prove Him and His Word. There are so many precious promises that God has given us in His Word. If we would only trust Him and believe Him, we would have everything we need for this life. I have heard of people who mark God's promises in their Bible with the letter p for promise. Later they add another p to mean precious promise, because they have proved God on that promise. What is your need today? Need peace? Jesus says, *casting all your care upon him; for he careth for you.* (1 Peter 5:7) Do you believe Him? *Ye lust, and have not: ye kill, and desire to have, and cannot obtain: ye fight and war, yet ye have not, because ye ask not.* (James 4:2) So then let us conclude that faith is made up of our belief and expecting that what God says in His Word will happen. The proof of faith comes when we exercise it, and the things we hope for, found in His Word, come to pass.

Where Do We Get Faith?

Hopefully, after studying what faith is, we all want to know where to get more faith. Did you know that we are actually commanded to have faith? I would imagine all of us have heard the saying, *the just shall live by faith.* That phrase is found in three passages in the Scriptures: Romans 1:17, Galatians 3:11, and Hebrews 10:38. Notice it does not say that we might live by faith or that we have access to it, if we want it. The word *shall* is a command. Who are the just that live by faith? The just are those who have been declared innocent and just by accepting Jesus Christ as their Savior.

Actually, we can go a step further than being commanded to have faith and say that living without faith is sin. *For whatsoever is not of faith is sin.* (Romans 14:23b) In my life, I have been a habitual worrier since I was a child. I think part of it is due to a tumultuous childhood, which is no excuse by the way. My worrying can be a result of fear or lack of control over a situation. I came to realize that faith expects and hopes for the best, but fear expects the worst. So then, faith is the opposite of fear. When I understood that not exercising faith is a sin and worrying is actually a form of atheism, I asked the Lord to forgive me and help me. I must say, with the Lord's help, I have overcome my tendency to fret and worry.

So then, we are commanded to have faith, but where do we get it? To get anything you have to go to the source of what you are looking for. The Lord God is the source of everything. The Scripture says to look *unto Jesus the author and finisher of our faith.* (Hebrews 12:2a) The Lord Jesus is the author of faith, which means He created it. It is beyond wonderful that the same Lord that commands us to have faith provides it. This is easy to understand when we know that He is the object of our faith. The Lord God of this universe is the only perfect being! He is the only one who will never fail us. *He is the Rock, his work is perfect: for all his ways are judgment: a God of truth and without iniquity, just and right is he.* (Deuteronomy 32:4) The Lord God is the only person worthy of our faith and trust. He is also the only person who can give us faith and also, increase our faith.

We get our first dose of faith when we get saved. How do we come to Christ for salvation? The Father by His Spirit draws us to Himself. *No man can come to me, except the Father which hath sent me draw him: and I will raise him up at the last day.* (John 6:44) The Father through His Word convicts us of His existence, His love, and our need. When we are saved, God's Spirit comes to dwell in us. *Who hath sealed us, and given the earnest of the Spirit in our hearts.* (2 Corinthians 1:22) The producer and author of faith comes to dwell in us. So every born again Christian has the source of faith within them. We have only to tap into it! By the way, we also get love at salvation. 1 John Chapter 4 tells us that God is love. When we get saved, God through His Spirit comes to live in our lives. So then, love comes to live in us.

How Do We Increase Our Faith?

I can truly identify with the father in Chapter 9 of the book of Mark who cried out to the Lord with tears: *I believe; help thou mine unbelief.* (Mark 9:24b) I do not always trust the Lord like I should. This man's son was possessed with a demon since he was a small child. The father was distraught over the situation and desperate. He brought the son to Jesus for healing. I believe the man may have understood who Jesus was, but could not yet comprehend what He could do. It is also possible he knew Jesus was capable of healing, but not sure He would do it for him. Maybe he could not yet comprehend God's love.

After salvation our seed of faith grows in the soil of God's Word, fertilized with love! *So then faith cometh by hearing, and hearing by the Word of God.* (Romans 10:17) *Faith which worketh by love.* (Galatians 5:6b) Our faith increases as we study God's Word and learn more about Him. The more we know about Him, the more we love Him. *He that loveth not knoweth not God; for God is love.* (1 John 4:8) The more we love, the more we trust. One of the key characteristics of God is His great love for us. We can completely trust the Lord because He loves us perfectly. Remember I said that fear is the opposite of faith. When we love the Lord like we should and understand how much He loves us, fear leaves us. *There is no fear in love; but perfect love casteth out fear: because fear hath torment. He that feareth is not made perfect in love.* (1 John 4:18) The word perfect in this verse refers to maturity—maturity in Christ. Those who are fearful all the time are not mature in Christ and do not love Him like they should.

I have been in desperate situations so often, haven't you? It seems so easy to rely on ourselves or others to fix our problems. Why is it that we neglect the One who loves us the most? Most often it is because He is removed from our mind and we do not know His Word well enough to know Him well enough. It is sometimes difficult for us to read and study God's Word like we should. We lead busy lives today. It took me a long time in my life to establish a daily pattern of reading the Scriptures. The world, Satan, and our flesh fight us to read it! It is easy to pass over God's Word and stay away from it. We must be diligent and not neglect the Scriptures. When we do take time to read the Word, often we just read words and gain no real understanding. The thing we need the most, we neglect the most. We need to set a time each day that we will read God's Word. If we miss one day, pick it back up the next day. Read with intent to know the Lord better. The daily devotion guides that we often use are good, but they cannot replace digging into the Word.

The Gospels tell us so much about Jesus; they are a good starting place. The rest of the New Testament sets forth how to live our lives as Christians. The Old Testament shows us how God loved and dealt with His chosen people, the Jews; which often relates to how He deals with His people today—Christians. Once we begin to regularly study and search God's Word, we see Him and who He is. We also learn of all the promises He has made to us. *I am come that they might have life, and that they might have it more abundantly.* (John 10:10b) If Jesus just came to earth to die to save us, that would have been enough and more than we ever deserved. Yet, He has so much more for us!

Once we read and know all we can know about Him, what do we do with it? We use it and apply it to our lives. Is it not truly amazing that we can trust the God of this universe to take us to Heaven for all eternity, but we fail daily to trust Him on the trip! Our Father's kingdom is full of people like the old woman who died of hunger and cold, while her wealth lay hidden beneath her mattress. We have not, because we ask not, because we believe not!

What Is the Result of Having Faith?

Jesus Himself gives us an example of what great faith looks like in Matthew 8:5-10.

And when Jesus was entered into Capernaum, there came unto him a centurion, beseeching him, and saying, Lord, my servant lieth at home sick of the palsy, grievously tormented. And Jesus saith unto him, I will come and heal him. The centurion answered and said, Lord, I am not worthy that thou shouldest come under my roof: but speak the word only, and my servant shall be healed. For I am a man under authority, having soldiers under me: and I say to this man, Go, and he goeth; and to another, Come, and he cometh; and to my servant, Do this, and he doeth it. When Jesus heard it, he marveled, and said to them that followed, Verily I say unto you, I have not found so great faith, no, not in Israel.

I do not know about you, but I want to have great faith in my life. So I studied and searched this passage to see what produced great faith in this man's life. What did you notice about this centurion? What in this passage speaks to his great faith? I noticed first his humility before the Lord. He was a ranking Roman soldier, yet he said that he was not worthy that Jesus should even come into his home. In addition, he recognized Jesus' authority. He obviously knew who Jesus was, because he sought Him out. He also knew Jesus' power, because he knew that Jesus would only have to speak and the servant would be healed. The centurion did not need a sign; he did not need Jesus to come to the servant; he had faith enough to believe that if Jesus said it, it would be so! Jesus did indeed heal the servant.

The centurion's love is what moved him to action on behalf of his servant. It is obvious to me that the centurion loved his servant. This was not just a case of a man who did not want to lose a servant he had paid for. Notice his statement concerning the servant: *he lieth at home sick of the palsy, grievously tormented.* The statement shows he wanted healing to remove the suffering. When you love, you want to remove the suffering of others. He sought out Jesus and he asked, because he knew that Jesus could help. The simple answer to what is great faith—believing who Jesus is and believing His Word. So then faith produces works in our life.

Even so faith, if it hath not works, is dead, being alone. Yea, a man may say, Thou hast faith, and I have works: shew me thy faith without thy works, and I will shew thee my faith by my works. (James 2:17-18)

Faith that does not move us to action is dead and useless. *For as the body without the spirit is dead, so faith without works is dead also.* (James 2:26) The definition for works in these passages from the book of James, is *to toil*. Toil for who or what? We toil for Jesus and others. Jesus' main purpose on this earth was to seek and to save the lost. Every work we do for Him should be an outflow of that purpose: telling others, loving others, and doing what we can to help. Faith and works produced by faith are so very important, but the Scripture tells us love is greater. *And now abideth faith, hope, charity, these three; but the greatest of these is charity.* (1 Corinthians 13:13) First Corinthians Chapter 13 says we can speak kindly like an angel; teach with all knowledge; have faith that can move a mountain; give everything to the poor; and sacrifice our own lives; but if it is not motivated by love, it is nothing. Love has to be the motivation behind exercising our faith—love for Jesus and others. The unsaved will not know we are Christians by our faith or our works, but by our love! *By this shall all men know that ye are my disciples, if you have love one to another.* (John 13:35)

The beginning of Hebrews Chapter 11 supplied our definition of faith. The rest of the chapter reveals very good examples of believers who showed us how to put faith and love into action.

By faith Abel offered unto God a more excellent sacrifice than Cain. (Hebrews 11:4a) Abel's sacrifice was more excellent than Cain's, because it was the kind of sacrifice that God required, a firstling of his flock. Abel's faith caused him to obey God completely.

By faith Noah, being warned of God of things not seen as yet, moved with fear, prepared an ark to the saving of his house. (Hebrews 11:7a) Noah built an ark on dry land and had faith that enough water would come from the sky to float it, when it had not rained before. The people of the day probably thought he was off his rocker.

Noah's faith caused him to believe God's Word, regardless of the fact that he had no historical or physical proof that a flood could come. Noah believed that God could do anything and his family was spared as a result.

By faith Abraham, when he was called to go out into a place which he should after receive for an inheritance, obeyed; and he went out, not knowing whither he went. (Hebrews 11:8) Abraham was called to leave his family and go to a place that had not been revealed to him yet. Abraham trusted God enough to leave the safety and security of his family to go to lands and people he did not know. God blessed him for it. If Abraham had not trusted and believed God, he would have missed all that God had for him.

Hebrews Chapter 11 goes on for forty verses naming hero after hero and describing their faith. Verse 39 brings the chapter to a close stating that *these all, having obtained a good report through faith.* They pleased God because they loved and trusted Him—their actions revealed it.

In a new Christian's life the first work that our new faith and love produces is telling our family and friends about Jesus. As a young Christian, I knew nothing except that I was saved and I had a letter from my God that would tell me everything I needed to know to live this Christian life. One of the most important subjects to me was the matter of people getting saved. In my child-like faith, I truly could not comprehend the possibility of people not getting saved, if Christians had the burden, prayed specifically for individuals, and the unsaved heard the Gospel. I truly believed that *with God all things are possible*! I still believe God can do anything.

One of my greatest burdens when I was first saved was for my dad. Out of respect for my dad I will not go into detail about his life, except to say that from a teenager he was in bondage to various substances that led to bouts of violent behavior. In 1983, during a violent time in my parents' home, I sought outside help for Dad's substance abuse problems and safety for my mother and sisters. In anger over my actions, my father expelled my husband, children, and myself from his life and forbade me contact with my mother and sisters. This exile lasted for ten long years. When I looked at my father's life, it seemed impossible for him to be saved.

In the spring of 1993, I received a call from my mother letting me know Dad had been diagnosed with stage four lung cancer. My heart fell because I could not comprehend him dying and going to Hell. By October of that year, Dad's health was quickly failing. Every time the phone rang I feared that it would be a call to let me know he was gone. Well-meaning Christian friends, who saw my grief and concern, lovingly told me that I had to understand that it was possible my dad would not get saved. I got angry every time I heard those words and decided that until he died, I would not give up praying and hoping that he would be saved. Is there anything God cannot do?

I will never forget November 5, 1993; it was a very rainy day. I was at my desk working and my pastor called and said he had been to visit my dad in the hospital that morning. He then asked me to come to the church, as he needed to speak to me in person. When I arrived at the church Pastor O'Neal and his wife, Anita, were waiting for me. I was immediately told that my dad had gotten saved that very morning. Tears of joy flooded my soul. I will never forget the moment or the feelings. In addition, our relationship was restored! To God be the glory, great things He hath done!!

Conclusion

Faith and love are so very important. This chapter is probably the most important in this book. I sincerely hope you learned something here. If nothing else, I hope you realized that faith and love are a dynamic duo! I also think we need to remember how important it is to teach our children that the Lord can be trusted. Our children will trust who we trust. As we grow as Christians and we learn more about Jesus, we need to share that information with our children. Each time the Lord proves Himself to you, please tell your children about it.

Perhaps as you read this chapter you realized you have never placed your trust in the Lord for salvation. Salvation determines how we will live this life and the next. Remember, a person who is in Christ is *a new creature; old things have passed away; behold all things have become new.* (2 Corinthians 5:17) Salvation does not bring perfection, but a new way of thinking and a new indwelling and presence of God in our lives. We need a Savior because we are sinners. *For all have sinned, and come short of the glory of God.* (Romans 3:23) A Savior who is the perfect, sinless Son of God, or God in the flesh. Without the Savior we will pay for our own sins by dying and going to Hell. *For the wages of sin is death; BUT the gift of God is eternal life.* (Romans 6:23) The Scriptures clearly teach that we have to *call upon the name of the Lord* (Romans 10:13a), and trust Him and Him alone to save and we *shall be saved.* (Romans10:13b) Dear friend, will you allow Jesus to save you today? I surely hope so.

For further help contact a local fundamental Bible preaching church in your area—or call or write

Victory Baptist Church, Inc. of James Island

335 Woodland Shores Road

Charleston, SC 29412

843-795-8229

Victory4charleston.org

Or email me at:

elainemichele2013@gmail.com

Chapter 3 Review

1. Breakdown Hebrews 11:1. Look up the important words and write their meaning.

    Faith—

    Substance—

    Things hoped for—

    Evidence—

    Things not seen—

2. See Hebrews 11:2. What was the good report that the elders obtained?

3. See Hebrews 11:4. Why was Abel's sacrifice more excellent than Cain's (Genesis 4)?

    What does faith have to do with the better sacrifice?

4. See Hebrews 11:6. Why is it impossible to please God without faith?

5. See Hebrews 11:13. What are some of the promises that these heroes of the faith had not received?

6. See Hebrews 11:22. What does faith have to do with Joseph asking for his bones to be moved?

7. See Hebrews 11:23-38. Name some of the ways that faith was displayed:

8. See Romans 10:17. Where does faith come from?

9. The day you accepted Christ as your personal Savior, how did you know to believe on the Lord and put your faith and trust in Him?

10. How does our faith increase in our Christian life?

11. See James 2:26. How do others see your faith?

Chapter 4

The Workshop of Faith: Marriage

Attempting to write about marriage in one chapter is like trying to put a seven course meal on one plate. There is too much content for the space! *Chopped* on the Food Network is one of my favorite shows. The most important part of that food competition is for contestants to include all of the contest ingredients on their final plate for the judges. My dilemma here is to choose the most important issues that affect a woman's married life. On the other hand, I think the better choice is to address foundational topics that will make our marriages strong and durable. It is always better to strengthen the foundation than to patch and dress up the structure.

The Lord **always** puts everything in perspective for me. He sweetly reminded me that if we do things His way, everything else falls into place. That is one lesson I have learned the hard way my entire Christian life. I want to do things my way and I get frustrated if things are not perfect. I am sure I am not alone in wanting to do things my way, because of Eve and her shenanigans! *For my thoughts are not your thoughts, neither are your ways my ways, saith the Lord.* (Isaiah 55:8) I think it takes a lot of faith for a woman to live the married life God's way and not the world's way. God's ways are perfect, ours are not. His thoughts are always for our best. Believing that God's way is the best and having faith in Him are the most important aspects of a successful marriage. In life our thoughts are often centered on what's best for us and not others, even our husband.

Selfishness does not work so well in life and especially in marriage. God tells us in several passages what His ways are concerning a woman and her relationship to her husband and her place in the marriage. We will look at those passages. The trouble is that many women want nothing to do with God's way in their marriages. I find that a very sad thought, since I know that God's ways for a marriage result in a little piece of Heaven on earth and the hope for living happily ever after! Not only do God's ways result in a little piece of Heaven on earth, but a host of all kinds of other good benefits for our children and other folks.

The alternative to God's way is not pretty or to be desired. Divorce is rampant in our society today among Christians and non-Christians. God said it was not to be so. I do not single out women or men as the fault of divorce; I blame both. It amazes me that people will follow all kinds of self-help techniques to make money, lose weight, stop aging, train children, etc., but they will not do anything effective to help their marriages. Have you ever heard an infomercial on a workshop to save failing marriages? I haven't, but I concocted one for you. Ladies, try the information presented in the Workshop of Faith to help save your failing marriage. Trust the Lord and apply information with His Word every day, without fail, money-back guarantee if you are not satisfied! Prove God!

Leave Our Baggage at the Door

Unfortunately, we are not perfect people and there are no perfect homes. We all are a product of some home, and possibly not a home where our parents knew Christ as their Savior. Even Christian homes are not perfect. In my case, I was raised in a non-Christian home until I married at age 17. I was not saved until age 28. I brought a lot of baggage into my marriage. Baggage can be sin, bad habits, prior wounds, and worldly ways. A man and a woman enter marriage as people who are a product of their past years of life. However, we do not have to be enslaved to those past years if we are in Christ.

Every day with Christ is a new day. *It is of the Lord's mercies that we are not consumed, because his compassions fail not. They are new every morning: great is thy faithfulness.* (Lamentations 3:22-23) The beginning of a marriage is like a new morning, a new start in a new life with our husbands. A good way to start that new life is by examining ourselves in the Lord and letting Him reveal those areas of our lives that need to be cleaned up or packed up and shipped out. When the Lord reveals sin we need to deal with it quickly, asking forgiveness and forsaking it. By the way, it is never too late to pack up that old baggage and ship it out! Actually packing up and shipping out sin and undesirable habits should be a lifelong practice.

Our home life as young people may have caused an accumulation of unwanted and undesirable baggage. For example, we may have come from a home where verbal abuse or the continual use of unkind and non-encouraging speech existed. The results of that type of environment can be two-fold: we may continue to practice that type of speech ourselves or we may lack confidence because we have been run down by that type of speech. God's Word is very specific about the kind of speech a Christian should not use. The Apostle Paul specifically lists the wrong kind of speech in Ephesians Chapters 4 and 5.

Let no corrupt communication proceed out of your mouth, but that which is good to the use of edifying, that it may minister grace unto the hearers. And grieve not the Holy Spirit of God, whereby ye are sealed unto the day of redemption. Let all bitterness, and wrath, and anger, and clamour, and evil speaking, be put away from you, with all malice. (Ephesians 4:29-31)

If we use these types of speech, we are in sin before God. We need to ask forgiveness, forsake it, and ask the Lord to help us overcome it. I mentioned earlier that Scripture memorization has always helped me. When I am tempted to sin I quote Scripture; I strike at the temptation with the sword of the Word of God. Remember to put off sinful speech; but replace it with godly speech, or that which encourages or improves the hearer.

Lacking self-confidence or feeling worthless due to past verbal abuse can sometimes be difficult to overcome. The best remedy and cure for these feelings is in God's Word. We need to remind ourselves that God loves us. *In this was manifested the love of God toward us, because that God sent his only begotten Son into the world, that we might live through him.* (1 John 4:9) He cared so much that He sent His only Son to die in our place. There is no greater love. If we can truly understand the extent to which God loves us, we can overcome anything. God not only loves us, but He cares about us and our daily lives. *Casting all your care upon him; for he careth for you.* (I Peter 5:7) When Satan comes and whispers those wrongful words from the past (and he will), we need to remind ourselves just how much God loves and cares for us.

Maybe the past abuse was more than just verbal. We hate to think of this as Christians, but physical abuse exists even in Christian homes. Any sin that an unsaved person can commit, a Christian can also commit. Physical abuse is often more difficult to overcome than verbal abuse. I think the most important factor in overcoming physical abuse is forgiving the person who committed the act. It is easy to hold hate and animosity towards those who hurt us physically, and even against those that could have prevented the harm. We need to learn to forgive and forget as Jesus does.

When we come to Jesus for salvation He forgives all our sin. *If we confess our sins, he is faithful and just to forgive us our sins, and to cleanse us from all unrighteousness.* (1 John 1:9) Actually, He blots them out, as if they never happened. *Repent ye therefore, and be converted, that your sins may be blotted out.* (Acts 3:19a) Blotting out is like they never existed. We are commanded to forgive others as

Christ forgave us. *Forbearing one another, and forgiving one another, if any man have a quarrel against any: even as Christ forgave you, so also do ye.* (Colossians 3:13) Forgiving those who have hurt us verbally and physically is a command. Those who say, "I will forgive, but I will never forget" have not really forgiven at all. Often traumatic incidences are hard to forget, but can be with the Lord's help. True forgiveness forgets the transgression. This means you can look at the person who committed the wrong and the wrong does not even come to mind. I know it can be done, because I have done it—but **only** with the help of the Lord.

We have to come to a place in our lives where we put our past behind us. The only way to accomplish that task is with the Lord's help through His Word. Forgive, forget, and follow Christ. *Stand fast therefore in the liberty wherewith Christ hath made us free, and be not entangled again with the yoke of bondage.* (Galatians 5:1) If we drag baggage into our married life, it will weigh us down and have a dampening effect on our new relationship. Anyone who drags around the baggage of their past will never go as far with Christ as He would intend for us. I do not know about you, but I want to go as far with Christ as I can in this life. The Apostle Paul said, *but this one thing I do, forgetting those things which are behind, and reaching forth unto those things which are before, I press toward the mark for the prize of the high calling of God in Christ Jesus.* (Philippians 3:13b-14)

I heard Dr. Cecil Beach preach a message in chapel to my son's senior class. As those seniors prepared to leave their high school days and enter college, Dr. Beach wanted them to leave their past behind. No matter what their lives had been up to that point, no matter what had happened, and no matter whether they had good or bad parenting, they were without excuse. We each have to stand before God and give an account one day. We will never be able to give the excuse that our sin, our choices, or our actions are the fault of someone else.

A Key to the House

I love weddings! The biggest joy of a wedding is the couple. When a man and woman start married life they are so much in love. In their minds they think their love cannot get any better than on the wedding day! They are so innocent and carefree. Little do they know is that their love will get stronger and deeper. The challenges and adjustments that will come are not even a thought on the wedding day. Old seasoned couples sit and watch the ceremony thinking, "You just don't know how your life will change!" Living happily ever after is all a couple contemplates as they enter marriage. The morning after the wedding, the couple awake to day one of the rest of their lives. He has morning breath and she has bed head—they realize the party is over! Or is the party just starting? I say the party of married life is just starting. However, it all depends on how we handle this new life and what we do for the rest of our life.

On day one of marriage the majority of folks have already forgotten the vows they made the day before. The standard vows always includes the part from God's Word that states the man and woman will leave mother and father and cleave together as one. What about the rest of the vow? Remember the part that says for better, for worse, in sickness, and in health, forsaking all others? There is not a specific verse that lays those words out in that manner, but the principle is certainly in Scripture. *[Love] beareth all things, believeth all things, hopeth all things, endureth all things.* (1 Corinthians 13:7) *Love is the fulfilling of the law.* (Romans 13:10b) Love is a key part of a successful marriage and home. Love for God first; then love for each other. Success for a Christian is measured by pleasing the Lord, receiving His blessings, and becoming more like Him. Marriage truly is the workshop where all of those things can happen.

We learned in Chapter 3 that when our love for the Lord is what it should be all else will fall into place. Love does conquer all. However, it has to be love that is God-based, because His is the only perfect love. We have to love as God loves—unconditionally.

We are fallible humans and the love we generate from our flesh is faulty, to say the least.

In the early years of marriage, love is often that fluffy, fuzzy stuff, more emotional than chosen. As the years pass, love moves more to a choice, even though the fuzzy feeling can still exist. The word love is both a noun and a verb. The thing called love is affection for someone or something. Love as a verb puts that affection into action by giving, caring, and doing for the ones we love.

Charity suffereth long, and is kind; charity envieth not; charity vaunteth not itself, is not puffed up, doth not behave itself unseemly, seeketh not her own, is not easily provoked, thinketh no evil; rejoiceth not in iniquity, but rejoiceth in the truth. (1 Corinthians 13:4-6)

Ladies, love your husbands with godly love. Godly love suffers or has long patience. Our husbands may have habits that annoy us—be patient. Our husbands may struggle with a particular sin—suffer long.

Godly love does not act with bitterness or resentment. We should not resent the tasks that are expected of us as wives. When we take care of our responsibilities out of love, they are never chores. When we have real love, we want to do for someone else, rather than having someone else to do for us.

Godly love does not boast of itself or exhibit pride. We should not boast when we conquer a certain sin or accomplish something we should be doing. Whenever we assert our good qualities or accomplishments, we are always setting ourselves above someone else.

Godly love does not behave in an unbecoming manner. Grabbing our husband's arm and escorting him to his seat when he is talking to a lovely church lady is not a good thing. Planting a long, sensual kiss on our husband in a public place is unbecoming of a Christian lady. Running our husbands down to others is improper.

Godly love always has the best interest of the other person in mind. Allowing our husband to choose the restaurant and even the meal plan is putting his interest before ours. Dressing warm when he has the thermostat set too cold is putting his comfort before ours.

Godly love is not annoyed or irritated. Do you ever get irritated picking up the clothes or the drinking glasses your husband leaves behind? I sometimes do! I heard a dear lady say that she lived her entire married life irritated at little things, like the clothes left on the floor. When her husband died, she said she would give anything to go back to picking up his clothes. We may one day long for those things that seem to irritate us today.

Godly love does not keep track of all the wrongs that are done. We should not keep lists of all the times our husband has hurt or wronged us. We may think we do not keep such lists; however, the true test comes when something happens and we can quickly and easily recall all the past wrongs.

Godly love does not rejoice when wrong is done or suffered. We should never be glad when our husband does something wrong even if it benefits our family. We should never take the attitude that someone is getting what they deserved when they suffer wrong.

Godly love always rejoices in truth. We should always be happy when truth prevails in our homes: truth in actions, truth in speech, and obeying the truth of God's Word. If we would love as God loves, our homes would be a much better place.

Pure godly love does not reside in our flesh, but we do have the Author of love living in us. The Scriptures tell us to *put on* certain qualities. If we naturally had these qualities we would not be told to put them on. We accomplish godly love in our lives when we put on *bowels of mercies, kindness, humbleness of mind, meekness, longsuffering; forbearing one another, and forgiving one another.* (Colossians 3:12b-13a) *And above all these things put on charity [love], which is the bond of perfectness.* (Colossians 3:14) A bond unites, controls, and keeps together. We walk with the Lord each day in

His Word, obeying the Word, and trusting Him to help us live this married life. I really believe in my heart that if both husband and wife loved as God loves, we would see no divorce—ever.

Safety at the Center of the House

Living in the south, we get severe thunderstorms from time to time. When a storm comes up that presents a tendency to create high winds, we get warnings from our local news station. The standard safety precautions are always the same—stay away from doors and windows and move to the center of your home. The center of the house is generally the safest and shields the family from breaking glass and flying debris. Jesus Christ should be the center of our lives, when we know Him as our Savior. He is the safest place to be in a marriage, whether during stormy or calm times.

Which hope we have as an anchor of the soul, both sure and steadfast. (Hebrews 6:19a) The Lord God is not only our safety, He is also our anchor. Have you ever seen how small the anchors are for huge ships? In comparison to the size of some ships, they seem inadequate to do the job, but they do! Our Lord God is big enough to handle any storm that comes our way. When a ship has its anchors down (no matter the type of seas), it stays in the place it is anchored to. The ship may sway from side to side and ride the high waves; but as long as that anchor is secure, it stays put. Jesus showed us how He protects in storms in the book of Mark. *And the same day, when the even was come, he saith unto them, Let us pass over unto the other side.* (Mark 4:35)

The first important point is that He told the disciples they would pass over to the other side. So often the Lord God gives us a promise from His Word and we do not trust it. Jesus intended to get to the other side with His disciples. I do not know anyone or anything that could prevent Jesus from doing what He intends to do. Do you?

And there arose a great storm of wind, and the waves beat into the ship, so that it was now full. And he was in the hinder part of the ship, asleep on a pillow: and they awake him, and say unto him, Master, carest thou not that we perish? And he arose, and rebuked the wind, and said unto the sea, Peace, be still. And the wind ceased, and there was a great calm. And he said unto them, why are ye so fearful? How is it that ye have no faith? (Mark 4:37-40)

Jesus had things under control. He knew they were going to the other side. The disciples had been with Jesus, watching all of His miracles. Why were they so fearful? Because they were just like we are; believing, but not trusting. Situations and storms arise; we look at the storm and forget what Jesus said, who He is, and how He loves and cares for us. Ladies, are you having trouble in your marriage? Are you even fearful it may fall apart? Is your anchor secure? Remember, it is God's will for marriages to stay together. God can turn a man's heart? *The king's heart is in the hand of the Lord, as the rivers of water: he turneth it whithersoever he will.* (Proverbs 21:1) I wish I could tell you how often I have seen the Lord turn my husband's heart. There were times before he was saved that I knew the Lord was leading me to do a certain thing that my husband would not agree to. Through prayer and a willingness to do what the Lord wanted, I saw miracles in my husband's responses.

And this is the confidence that we have in him, that, if we ask any thing according to his will, he heareth us: and if we know that he hears us, whatsoever we ask, we know that we have the petitions that we desired of him. (1 John 5:14-15)

We do not always know the Lord's will in some situations, but often we do. We know that it is not God's will for marriage to end except by the death of a partner. *What therefore God hath joined together, let not man put asunder.* (Matthew 19:6b) As long as we are anchored in and to the Lord and trusting Him, we can handle anything that comes our way—money-back guarantee.

The best way for a Christian woman to anchor herself to the Lord is to stay in His Word. We need to know Him and His Word. We need to find the answers to live our lives there. The answers we need in our marriage are never found in the world. Talk to the Lord in prayer and let Him talk to you through His Word. If we truly want to know what the Lord says about any matter, He will show us. *Ask, and it shall be given you; seek, and ye shall find; knock, and it shall be opened unto you.* (Matthew 7:7) Not only do we need to know His Word, we need to trust His Word. Only Trust Him, now! *For he hath said, I will never leave thee, nor forsake thee.* (Hebrews 13:5b)

Keep Your House in Order

While it is important for us to keep our house in physical order, there is a more important aspect of order that we need to know as women. The Lord God has a chain of command that He has established for the home and many times it is not followed. The world is the biggest protestor of God's chain of command and Christian women are slowly falling in behind them. *For the husband is the head of the wife, even as Christ is the head of the church.* (Ephesians 5:23a) God's chain of authority is Himself first, then the husband, and then the wife. If you are practicing this order, it does not sound so bad; if you are not, it sounds horrid. Our human nature naturally rebels against authority. There has to be an order of command. If there is not, confusion and duplication of responsibilities occurs.

God never said that a man is better than a woman. In fact, the Apostle Peter states that the husband and wife are *heirs together of the grace of life.* (1 Peter 3:7b) When man and woman marry, they are one flesh. To submit to our husbands is really serving our own flesh in multiple ways. God created men and women diverse to assume different roles. When those roles are not followed, things are just not right. God primarily created men to lead and to toil in work. God primarily created women to help their husbands, bear children, and to nurture. God has an order for everything.

It would appear as though woman came under the rule of man after Eve sinned. God told Eve, *I will greatly multiply thy sorrow and thy conception; in sorrow thou shalt bring forth children; and thy desire shall be to thy husband, and he shall rule over thee.* (Genesis 3:16) Many women think that they are suffering Eve's punishment by being under the rule of their husband. I am not so sure that is true. God created Adam first, then Eve. God evidenced an order of authority with the man and woman when He created them. If you will notice, God perfectly designed men and women to fulfill different roles, even before they sinned. Just as God has an order for all things in His creation, He created an order for men and women. Without order, nothing operates and functions as it should. I want to restate that God never indicates that men are better than women. He never indicates that He loves or cares for men more than women. It is just order by plan and design.

Long ago in our church, our pastor's wife, Mrs. Anita, set out to teach the women about God's order in the home. She would tell us, "If you let him be the king, he will let you be the queen." This is so true. If we submit and let our husband fill the role God intended, he will be more apt to treat us like his queen. I thank the Lord for Mrs. Anita as a godly mentor. I needed a lot of help in this area. My home life as a young person was complete turmoil. As a result of my first 17 years of life in pure survival mode, I was a very independent person. When I married, my independence (baggage) came along with me into my marriage.

God intends for men to lead in their home and normally men expect that leadership to exist. In the early years of marriage, both husband and wife are adjusting to the newness of everything associated with married life. In those years of marital bliss men will overlook a non-submissive wife. However, as time passes and both begin to settle in, similar to a new house settling, the issues begin to appear and stand out.

Even before I was saved, I felt to be a good wife I needed to attend to my husband's every need, so I did everything I thought that entailed. In addition to working outside of the home, I cooked, cleaned, took care of the finances, and the lists goes on and on. In all of these great works, I failed in a key component and that was submitting to his authority as my husband. Good works and obedience in many areas never substitute for disobedience in another area. I am ashamed to say that when I got saved the submitting did not happen immediately or easily. We have that old nature inside us, that tendency to do things our way and not the Lord's way. God has established the order of authority, but we have to follow it.

Submission has become a word that invokes uncomfortable feelings in women. Submission goes against our fleshly nature, because we want to do what we want to do. However, submitting is a part of our entire life. We submit to our boss at work, the government, the police, teachers, just to name a few. Again, we see God has an order to everything. Most of all, we should be submitting to the Lord and to our husbands. Submission is willingly placing one's self under the authority of another.

Wives, submit yourselves unto your own husbands, as unto the Lord. (Ephesians 5:22) I think if we would remember while submitting or during our failure to do so, that we are submitting to the Lord, we would have a different attitude. Attitude is the bulk of it. Bottom line, when we do not submit to our husbands, we are disobeying the Lord. We need to let our husbands lead in the home. Do what he asks and even what he does not ask, if you know it should be done. Do not do things against his wishes, even if you think it needs to be done. I always make sure I do what my husband asks as quickly as possible. I have a list in the front of my Bible that reminds me of the things I regularly need to do. Really the list is just little things: have supper on time; pay the bills as he requires; keep the house and laundry clean. Many of the tasks are things we women would do whether we were married or single. Often women will not do tasks just to irritate the husband, or to proclaim they will not submit. When we fight against submitting to our husbands, life will be hard, like rowing against the current.

I noticed a long time ago that the Scripture does not give us a release from submission if our husbands are not acting or behaving the way they should. Each person has to give an account to the Lord one day for their own actions. In addition, submission should never be used as a tool to manipulate our husbands. Submission protects us against not overloading ourselves with things other people outside of our home want us to do. Our first and foremost responsibility is to our husbands and our homes. There is only **one** exception to not submitting to our husband and that would be if he demands that we do something that causes us to personally sin against the Lord. *We ought to obey God rather than men.* (Acts 5:29b)

Warren Wiersbe says that submission is also an opportunity. First, it can be an opportunity to win an unsaved husband to the Lord. *Likewise, ye wives, be in subjection to your own husbands; that, if any obey not the word, they also may without the word be won by the conversation of the wives.* (1 Peter 3:1) *Conversation* in this verse means *our walk and our actions.* Notice that the verse says the husband is won *without the word,* which does not mean without the Word of God. We know that salvation only comes through believing by the Word of God. The husband may be won without our spoken word. So nagging and pestering your husband to be saved is not allowed—it does not work!

Submission is a super important issue when you have an unsaved husband. Submitting can really melt a cold heart! I know, I was saved 17 years before my husband. The Lord used the book of 1 Peter, among other Scriptures, during that entire time to help me. Submission is an opportunity to encourage and strengthen our saved husband in the Lord. Another opportunity that sweet submission gives is being a good testimony to our children, especially our daughters. Our children really do pay more attention to what we do, rather than what we say. A daughter who is raised in a home where the mother does not submit or rules the home, will more than likely repeat the same patterns. A sweet spirit of submission will be a testimony to many, including friends and family.

Submission is also an outward adorning or decoration. It is compared to clothing, makeup, and jewelry that a woman would put on. This type of adorning comes from the inside out.

Whose adorning let it not be that outward adorning of plaiting the hair, and of wearing of gold, or of putting on of apparel. But let it be the hidden man of the heart, in that which is not corruptible, even the ornament of a meek and quiet spirit, which is in the sight of God of great price. (1 Peter 3:3-4)

A meek and quiet spirited woman who sweetly submits to her husband is of great price to the Lord. Often some will use this passage to mean women should not wear makeup or jewelry. The Apostle Peter is not saying that at all. A woman's real beauty comes from her nature, the way she behaves, and the way she handles herself. As Christian women, we should look our best. Makeup and jewelry can and should be tasteful and discreet. Every man is proud of an attractive wife. We will address this particular topic more in the next chapter.

Finally, submission to the Lord and our husbands puts a woman under an umbrella of protection. I do not know about you, but I want to be protected. *Even as Sara obeyed Abraham, calling him lord: whose daughters ye are, as long as ye do well, and are not afraid with any amazement.* (1 Peter 3:6) The word *afraid* refers to being *frightened or alarmed.* A Christian woman who develops a meek and quiet spirit of submission never has to fear anything. The protection that a husband's leadership provides is so very important. A husband protects the wife by leading in family decisions. I do not know about you, but major decisions are stressful to me. A husband can quickly and easily make important decisions, because God created him to do so. Often emotions affect a woman's ability to make decisions, but not men. This is why men can go to war and kill if it is necessary.

A husband physically protects by providing shelter and food for his family. A husband spiritually protects his family by leading them to church and in the study of God's Word. You may say, "My husband is not doing those things. Why should I submit to him?" Submission is obedience to the Lord and obedience to the Lord brings protection from the Lord. *Ye shall walk in all the ways which the Lord your God hath commanded you, that ye may live, and that it may be well with you.* (Deuteronomy 5:33a) I can think of many benefits that I receive from submitting to my husband. The benefit I treasure the most is peace in my life. The world is desperately trying to make women think they do not need men, nor need to submit to them. Many times our family and friends, especially the unsaved, will not support our efforts to be a submissive wife. However, we must press on, for when we do, we please the Lord.

Those who are single still have a duty of submission. As I previously stated, God has an order for all of life. A woman who is not married still has men in her life that she needs to submit to, namely her father, step-father, or grandfather. As a woman matures and is out on her own, the father's role will become a leadership role more than a role of direct authority. Submitting to the father affords much protection for an unmarried woman. If a woman has no one in the position of a father, other godly male family members can take that role. Scripture reminds us that Esther was orphaned and taken in by her cousin Mordecai. *And he brought up Hadassah, that is, Esther, his uncle's daughter: for she had neither father nor mother.* (Esther 2:7a) The Women's Libbers of this world will not like this next statement, but it is true for a Christian woman. A Christian woman without male leadership is like a turtle without a shell—vulnerable.

The "S" Word

I promise this section will be quick and painless for both of us. As a general rule, the topic of sex is not discussed very often among Christian women. I truly understand why, but feel that it is a necessary topic, because there is a lot of false information coming from the world. Obviously, we need to discuss sex and its physical aspects with our daughters. The Lord God created sex by virtue of the way He physically created men and women. Sex is not just for making babies; it is a vital part of the relationship between husband and wife. Unfortunately, the world has grossly made sex a dirty act. The world has also made a very private relationship very public.

Before we go on, let us identify sexual relationships that God does not approve of. Adultery is sex with someone other than a marriage partner. *Thou shalt not commit adultery.* (Exodus 20:14) Fornication is sex before marriage. *Flee fornication. Every sin that a man doeth is without the body; but he that committeth fornication sinneth against his own body.* (1 Corinthians 6:18) Homosexuality is sex with a person of the same sex. *If a man also lie with mankind, as he lieth with a woman, both of them have committed an abomination.* (Leviticus 20:13a) *And likewise also the men, leaving the natural use of the woman, burned in their lust one toward another; men with men working that which is unseemly, and receiving in themselves that recompense of their error which was meet.* (Romans 1:27) These practices of sex are condemned by God as sin. Unfortunately, these practices are rampant in our world today. So much so that all people, many Christians included, have come to accept that they are okay.

Sex fulfills a need for both the husband and the wife. Men need sex mostly to fill a physical need; while women need sex to fill an emotional need. Generally men need sex more often than women. Often because of the responsibilities that women have in the home and with the children, by days end we women are physically tired. Our husband may come in from work with that look in his eyes. You know what I am talking about. All we can think of is a hot bath and a long night's sleep! Ladies, do what it takes to meet the physical needs of your husband, not begrudgingly, but with a sweet spirit. Even when he does not have that look in his eye, pay attention. Do not let his needs go unfulfilled. Long ago, I heard a dear Christian lady speaking on the radio. She said, "For every time we have a headache (to avoid sex), there is a woman out in the world with an aspirin willing to take our husbands."

Nevertheless, to avoid fornication, let every man have his own wife, and let every woman have her own husband. Let the husband render unto the wife due benevolence: and likewise also the wife unto the husband. The wife hath not power of her own body, but the husband: and likewise also the husband hath not power of his own body, but the wife. Defraud (keep back) *ye not one the other, except it be with consent for a time, that ye may give yourselves to fasting and prayer; and come together again, that Satan tempt you not for your incontinency.* (1 Corinthians 7:2-5)

Ladies, even the godliest men are tempted. We need to be on guard with our husbands and take care of all their needs. We need to dress for our husband to show him we are happy to see him at the end of his work day. When he comes home daily to us in sweats or comfortable clothes, no makeup, and hair undone, after a while those nicely dressed ladies at the office begin to look appealing. I think most women are naturally beautiful. An attractively dressed lady with her hair fixed may not need makeup. However, some of us need a little beauty from a jar!

A handsome groom and a very beautiful bride stood at the alter one day. The bride was stunning, of course as every bride should be, with her long flowing hair and sparkling eyes. In the wee hours of the next morning that beautiful bride quietly got up and removed all of her makeup and pulled her hair up. She quietly slipped back in bed next to her new husband. A few hours later the handsome groom awoke. He pulled the covers up to his chin and started screaming, "Who are you and what have you done with my wife!"

Moral of this story: Ladies, we only need a **little** beauty from a jar. In the early years of marriage, we generally pay closer attention to taking care of ourselves. However, the longer we are married we become more relaxed and unconcerned about our appearance, and maintaining a strong emotional and physical relationship with our husbands.

One day, the children will be grown, the responsibilities will lessen, and we will sit across the room from our husbands and wonder what do we do now? If we have kept the emotional and physical relationship alive, our marriages will only become sweeter. *Marriage is honourable in all, and the bed undefiled: but whoremongers and adulterers God will judge.* (Hebrews 13:4)

Happily Ever After

My son's church has an annual sweetheart banquet in February to celebrate Valentine's Day. In 2014, the banquet featured each couple pictured holding a sign that read *Happily Ever After.* My son Rob Fipps and his wife Trisha looked as radiant in their banquet picture as they did on their wedding day twelve years ago. Are their lives perfect? Certainly not perfect. Do they face trials and tribulations? Yes, just like all Christians do. Jesus told us we would have trials and tribulations in this world. *These things I have spoken to you, that in me ye might have peace. In the world ye shall have tribulation: but be of good cheer; I have overcome the world.* (John 16:33) Jesus promises to never leave us and He will see us through to the end. One practice that my son and his wife have continued through their marriage impresses me. They always strive to keep their relationship strong. Rob and Trisha both do little things for the other, like leaving notes in unsuspecting places. Special events like birthdays and anniversaries are always made to be very exceptional. Date night is a constant activity that they share. The importance of all this is that they actively pursue strengthening their marriage relationship. We should do the same. This is a key part of living happily ever after.

All of the women I know would want to live happily ever after. How about you? So just how do we do that? Imagine, if you would, a couple riding a two-seated bike. The husband is driving and they are out riding together on a beautiful sunny day. The breeze is cool and the flowers are fragrant. The husband is following a path that the Lord has laid out for him and his bride. Along the ride the couple hit a few bumps, but together they keep the bike aright. The husband has to swerve a few times to avoid a mishap, but the wife sweetly follows along. Pedestrians hear the couple singing sweetly as they ride by. The husband's voice is stronger, since he is in the lead. The wife's voice softly echoes her husband's refrain. The couple never looks back, because they are focused on their destination. At some points the path is steep, but the strong husband works hard to pull the two up the path. It begins to rain, but only the husband gets wet because he is shielding the wife. At the end of their journey the couple arrives together safely at their destination. They are barely exhausted because they pedaled the bike together. The journey would not have been the same had the couple been on two separate bikes!

We live happily ever after when:

We keep Christ at the center of our lives.

We follow God's chain of command in our lives.

We love as God loves.

We obey God's commands.

We put the past behind us.

Amen!

Chapter 4 Review

1. What kind of emotional baggage could a woman bring into a marriage?

2. When the Lord saves us, what does He do with all of our sin baggage? (See Psalm 103:12)

3. Do you think it is possible to put our past behind us?

4. Can you give a Scripture that would help us with this?

5. When a woman gets married where is the best place for her to place her faith as she starts her new life?

6. Do you think marriage really is a workshop for faith? If yes, why?

7. Read Hebrews 6:19. Do you think a marriage anchored in the Lord can be steadfast and sure?

8. Please choose one word that you think should be the key to any home.

9. In 1 Corinthians 13:4, *Charity (love) suffereth long.* Can you give an example of suffering long?

10. In 1 Corinthians 13:5, *Charity (love) seeketh not her own.* What does this mean?

11. In 1 Corinthians 13:5, *Charity (love) thinketh no evil.* Name one area that it may be easy to think evil of your mate.

12.   Does love really conquer all?

13.   Read Ephesians 5:22-24. List God's chain of command in a
      married woman's life.

14.   Look up the words submit and submission and define them.

15.   In Scripture what is the difference between the sin of
      fornication and the sin of adultery?

16.   Read 1 Corinthians 7:1-5. If husbands and wives abstain
      from sex, how can they be tempted by Satan?

17.   Does God intend for our marriages to last forever?

18.   Give me a verse to prove your answer above.

19.   If you were asked to name one thing that contributes to all
      divorce, what do you think would it be?

Chapter 5

A Christian Woman's Realm

Up to this point, the information contained in this book has been very foundational. This chapter and the next will be more practical. I start this chapter with a discussion on taking care of ourselves individually. Our behavior, actions, and usefulness in our home, our church, and the world stem from how we care for ourselves. It is very important for women to know how to handle day to day situations in every realm of life.

The most important aid in our daily lives is to trust in the Lord and knowing His Word. It is so important to start our day with prayer. I can tell it really makes a difference for me. If I had to choose (and I hope I never do) I would rather pray than put on makeup! It is a choice of being ugly on the inside or the outside! If I fail to pray, I feel that I have left something off! When we pray to the Lord we are acknowledging His presence in our lives. We are also taking time to be with Him first, before other responsibilities. We can lay our burdens on Him and tell Him about our day ahead. I always ask Him to help me be kind and loving to those around me. I also ask that He help me filter my duties for the day, so I will set aside things that are unnecessary and not waste time. Prayer is so important, but so easily neglected.

As women, our lives revolve around dealing with our homes, our churches, and the world. We need to know how we fit in those places and just what our responsibility is and what it is not. I have a very dear friend who is going through a difficult time. Her husband is not leading, supporting, or caring for their home. What would we do in that situation? I know Christian women right now who are confused as to their roles in their local churches. Scripture has the answers. How do we witness and show love to the unsaved and not participate in worldly activities? All of these situations are things we deal with on a regular basis. Scripture has the answers, but often we do not know where to find what we are looking for. I hope we can learn together how to deal with our daily situations, as we delve into a Christian woman's realm.

Me and Myself

This section's subtitle sounds self-centered, but I think it is very important for a woman to take good care of herself. We need to be sure we are well-balanced and in good shape spiritually, emotionally, and physically. Actually, if we are off in any one of these areas, we can be off in the other areas as well. We women lead very busy lives; it is very easy to neglect ourselves, as we put others first. Obviously, the first area of concern needs to be the spiritual part of us. Be sure to make time daily for prayer and Bible study—the first part of the day, if at all possible. This may mean getting up a little earlier for a tired momma, but it is well worth it.

1 Thessalonians 5:17 says, *pray without ceasing*. Praying without ceasing is staying in an attitude of prayer. We can do that more easily if we start the day with prayer. Several years ago my husband decided we needed to get up at 4:30 a.m. so he could have time to pray and do devotions before he left for work at 5:30. At that time, I prayed and did devotions after he left for work. I wish I could say that I was thrilled about his new desire, but I was not. To this day, I still have a hard time rolling out when the clock rings. However, I have to say that it is well worth it. It is such a precious time to start our mornings with prayer and Bible study. When my husband, or

anyone else in my family for that matter, wants to make an effort to grow in the Lord, I should never prevent it.

You may not have much time to commit to prayer and reading in the mornings, but please do it for some amount of time. Even if you only read a few verses, meditate on those verses and break them down as to what they mean to you. We should talk to the Lord every chance we get, even while in the shower or doing the dishes. I pray while driving! We have to pray these days; the byways are crazy. When we make prayer and Bible reading a part of our daily life, it will be much easier to turn to them when we really need it. By the way, we may not think this too often, but we *really* need prayer and the Bible every day. The virtuous woman of Proverbs 31:26 *openeth her mouth with wisdom; and in her tongue is the law of kindness.* Real wisdom comes from the Lord and spending time with Him and His Word. *The fear of the Lord is the beginning of wisdom: a good understanding have all they that do his commandments: his praise endureth forever.* (Psalm 111:10)

It also does not hurt to regularly take a spiritual inventory of our lives. I love to use David's prayer from Psalm 139 to ask the Lord to let me know where I need to change. *Search me, O God, and know my heart: try me, and know my thoughts: And see if there be any wicked way in me, and lead me in the way everlasting.* (Psalm 139:23-24) When the Lord convicts us of sin, we need to address it quickly and not let it pile up like dirty laundry. Keep a short account with the Lord. *If we confess our sins, he is faithful and just to forgive us our sins, and to cleanse us from all unrighteousness.* (1 John 1:9) Remember, we need to do more than just confess our sins, we need to forsake them. Also, when temptation does come, be quick to nip it in the bud. We always have a way to escape.

There hath no temptation taken you but such as is common to man: but God is faithful, who will not suffer you to be tempted above that ye are able; but will with the temptation also make a way to escape, that ye may be able to bear it. (1 Corinthians 10:13)

I always think of an escape hatch when I read this verse. Jesus is our escape hatch. We should run to Him when we are tempted. Temptation can be hard sometimes. Our old flesh likes its old and worldly ways. We run to Jesus through His Word. When Jesus was tempted He quoted Scripture to Satan. *But he answered and said, it is written, man shall not live by bread alone, but by every word that proceedeth out of the mouth of God.* (Matthew 4:4) If quoting Scripture was what Jesus did, I think it is good enough for us. Scripture memory is like sharpening our sword. It makes us ready like a solider when the battle comes. It is our only defense against the enemy. If we do not know Scripture, we are like a city with no walls. We are defenseless!

Satan's main battle ground is our minds, so above all we need to guard them. Our minds are where everything begins. Every sin starts with a thought. *For as he thinketh in his heart, so is he.* (Proverbs 23:7a) So often I kneel to pray and so many other things come into my mind. Some are not good. I am easily distracted during prayer time. If Satan can interrupt our prayer time and Bible study, he can defeat us. Knowing Scripture is the best way to battle Satan, but we also need to build a strong mind for the Lord. The way we do this is to be filled with the Word of God and the Spirit of God. *Walk in the Spirit, and ye shall not fulfil the lust of the flesh.* (Galatians 5:16b)

But be filled with the Spirit; speaking to yourselves in psalms (the Word) *and hymns and spiritual songs, singing and making melody in your heart to the Lord; giving thanks always for all things unto God and the Father in the name of our Lord Jesus Christ.* (Ephesians 5:18b-20)

I do not know about you, but my mind is a much better place when I have a spiritual song in my heart and an attitude of gratitude. We are filled with the Spirit of God when we do not have unconfessed sin in our lives, are obeying God's commands, and letting Him lead in our lives. Accomplishing this (to me) sounds like trying to chew gum and walk at the same time. However, the same Lord God that commands us to be filled with the Spirit helps us to do this. If we set our hearts and minds to be filled with the Spirit, we can do it with the Lord's help. When we desire to obey the Lord and follow Him, He always helps. Unfortunately, we believers generally want to follow our own ways.

When we are filled with God's Word and His Spirit, it also produces peace in our minds. *And let the peace of God rule in your hearts, to which also ye are called in one body; and be ye thankful.* (Colossians 3:15) We need peace in our minds, because our minds are the center of our emotions. What we think about situations affects our emotional responses. Women are very emotional creatures. When we have peace and stability in our minds, our emotions (which lead to our actions) tend to be in check. Happiness and joy rarely cause any ill actions. However, it is the negative emotions that cause us to behave in an unbecoming manner.

Think about some of the negative feelings with which we deal: anger, hurt, indignation, guilt, and fear. Anger, hurt, and indignation very often stem from wounded pride. Guilt comes from situations that we feel could have been handled better or that we failed in. Guilt often is a big issue for women because of all the responsibilities we have. Often steeped in pride, guilt is a big problem for me. My pride desires that I do all things perfectly. I am here to tell you, it is impossible to do all things perfectly. Jesus was the only perfect person to ever walk this planet. We need to do the best we can and leave the rest to the Lord.

What about fear? I think women can also be very fearful. Remember we discussed fear in Chapter 3; it is the opposite of faith (or trusting). When we allow any of these feelings to swell in our minds, they often push us to bad behavior and poor choices. In addition, these emotions can immobilize us! May I suggest a solution: Stop, drop, and roll! Yes, we are putting out a fire—the fire of a woman on an emotional charge. Stop it!! Do not allow yourself to wallow in bad emotions. Drop to your knees and ask the Lord to help. Roll on to the next thing in life; quickly put things behind you.

Our minds are like Grand Central Station; one train moves out and another moves in. The station is always filled with a hub bub of people. The schedule is always rolling on for more trains. It is a wonder we can get our minds to calm down to rest. We have a lot to think about with all of our daily tasks and duties as women. It can be very easy to let the busyness of life overwhelm and stress us. I will use the Apostle Paul's terminology when I say I am a chief sinner, especially in the area of worrying and fretting over duties and tasks. I am a doer. I am always worried about getting my doing done, when I am not relying on the Lord.

Be careful for nothing; but in everything by prayer and supplication with thanksgiving let your requests be made known unto God. (Philippians 4:6) The word *careful* in this verse means *anxious*. We are to be anxious about **nothing**! Jesus told Michele (uh, I mean Martha), *thou art careful* (anxious) *and troubled about many things: but one thing is needful: and Mary hath chosen that good part, which shall not be taken away from her.* (Luke 10:41-42) What is the good part? Sitting at the feet of Jesus, beholding Him, and listening to Him. That is the **only** place of rest and peace in our busy lives.

Years of worry and stress will leave us with physical problems. I truly believe that stress is a killer and a main factor in many illnesses today. We need to take care of our bodies. When we are saved our bodies are the temple of God. Only God knows when our lives will end. Until the end, we need to take care of our body as if we may live to be over 100! Eat well. Really, it does not take much thought as to what we should or should not eat. The problem is we want to eat what we want. We know what is good and bad when it comes to food. Rest well. Get the proper rest for your body. Sometimes, it is more spiritual to leave the dirty dishes and go to bed. Run from time wasters. Sitting up in front of the television, playing Candy Crush, or checking Facebook will not profit one ounce in our walk with Christ. Stay active. A body in motion does stay in motion.

As women, we do need to be balanced physically, emotionally, and spiritually. Being balanced means we are stable and steady. We do not achieve balance by doing everything well and with perfection. We achieve balance by having Jesus Christ as the center of our lives. Every day we should do what we can, the best we can, leaving the rest to Jesus. Do not look back; do not contemplate; and do not fret. We can only change today and tomorrow with the Lord's help.

In Our Home

The home is the most important place on earth for the Christian family. After the crucifixion of Christ, His disciples were sad, confused, and fearful. *Then the disciples went away again unto their own home.* (John 20:10) Home is the place we go for solace, comfort, encouragement, and love. Home is our main place of learning. Inside the walls of our home is a physical place of protection from the world. Christ is or should be the center of our home. Everything should revolve around the Lord and His Word. The father is the protector and provider of the home, while the mother is the builder and nurturer of the home. We have already discussed God's order of command in the home. The husband is the head of the home, the wife, and the children. The wife is the husband's help-meet, the vice-president or assistant manager if you will. She is also a keeper of the home. A keeper of the home is a guard of the home or someone aware of all that goes on in the home. Keepers or guards never leave their post or assignment. A woman's assignment is her home and her family.

All issues that affect the home are the ultimate and direct responsibility of the husband, the captain of the guard, who should be under the control of the Lord. It is important to know how this structure actually works in the home in day-to-day life. Many women wonder how they should function in their homes while allowing the husband to be in control. We addressed a lot of this in the last chapter, as we discussed the wife's submission to her husband. Each home is different and each husband is different. Some husbands do more than other husbands. Today it seems like young husbands are much more involved in doing things in the home. In my day, husbands did less in the home. My husband never changed diapers; however, my son and son-in-law change diapers all the time. Times do change, but the chain of command in the home does not.

The husband's preferences should always be honored first. This is because he is the head of the home and because the Bible admonishes it—*in honour preferring one another.* (Romans 12:10b) If there is an area where he has no preference, the wife makes the decision. I mentioned earlier that my husband likes to rise at 4:30 a.m. each workday. It is my responsibility to go with that schedule and to be up with him to start the day assisting with items he needs. Many husbands like supper ready when they get home from work or at a certain time each day. We need to do everything possible to comply. All husbands like to have clean clothes—who doesn't? So make sure laundry is a priority.

When there are decisions to be made about the home or the family, I always defer to my husband's decision. Where we live, go to church, school our children, and household finances all fall under the husband's responsibility. Often we discuss situations and I give my view, but ultimately my husband makes the decision. By the way, when you are submitting in a godly fashion, your opinion will be held in high regard. We may not always agree with our husband's decisions, but we always defer to him. No one else should ever know you disagree. It amazes me that my husband's decisions generally always work out better than what I would have done. If our husbands make a wrong decision we should never say *I told you so*. A tremendous weight is relieved from a woman who rests under the authority of her husband. There is much less to worry about when we fill our proper place in the home and do not take on things that are not under our authority. We need to pray for our husbands and the decisions they have to make—leading a home and a family is not an easy job. We should support our husbands always and in every situation we can. God forbid if a time ever comes that we cannot support what he is doing or a decision he makes, we still honor him and pray for him!

In a lot of homes the wife takes care of the finances. When the finances are our responsibility, we need to take care of them just like our husband would want and expect. *The heart of her husband doth safely trust in her, so that he shall have no need of spoil.* (Proverbs 31:11) The word spoil in this verse refers to *a bounty or a prey.* People are spoiled when someone comes into their homes and takes what they have or there is waste. Our husbands should never worry that we are wasting the family finances or using them inappropriately. Often a husband never sees the checkbook or the bills. Satan will tempt us to do what we want with the finances and sometimes spend where we should not. Remember God always sees everything. A good way to be accountable is to periodically prepare a report for our husbands as to the state of the finances or let him review the checkbook register. Also, if a problem arises where the bills cannot be paid, the wife should always bring this to the attention of the husband. A wife's duty with the finances is to be prudent, take good care, and not be wasteful. I would also recommend saving and investing when it is possible to do so, with our husband's permission. A good steward of finances is not only prudent and not wasteful; they also make honest gain when they can. *She considereth a field, and buyeth it: with the fruit of her hands she planteth a vineyard.* (Proverbs 31:16) The "Proverbs" woman was not only investing, but supplying fresh food for the family at a reduced cost.

There are many tasks to be taken care of in the home, many of which may fall on the wife. We need to take care of whatever duties are assigned to us with a good attitude. Did you know that attitude is the majority of our battle as we face daily life? *As ye have therefore received Christ Jesus the Lord, so walk ye in him: rooted and built up in him, and stablished in the faith, as ye have been taught, abounding therein with thanksgiving.* (Colossians 2:6-7) Our outlook on life affects every part of our daily routine! The outlook that produces the best outcome is an attitude of gratitude!

A wife sets the tone or mood in her home. The old saying, *If momma ain't happy, nobody ain't happy,* is absolutely true! I have learned in my life that nothing is automatic, which includes happiness and a good mood. The Scripture tells us over and over to put off and to put on. When I got saved I was under the false impression that we automatically do well and act right after salvation. That was very foolish and wishful thinking on my part. Boy, did I get a rude awakening! Establishing a good atmosphere in the home starts with putting Jesus first, then our husbands. We have to do this willingly and with a good attitude. Putting our authorities in their proper place should permeate the mood of the entire home and occupants.

Secondly, we have to put on some things. *Put on therefore, as the elect of God, holy and beloved, bowels of mercies, kindness, humbleness of mind, meekness, longsuffering.* (Colossians 3:12) Bowels of mercies is lovingly being sympathetic to those around you. Kindness is being kind and thoughtful. Humbleness of mind is being humble in thought and action. Humility always esteems others first. Meekness and longsuffering is gentleness and patience. Ladies, if we would put on these characteristics, *as the elect of God,* our homes would be such a pleasant place. Putting on and putting off is a choice. We have to work at this and be alert when our mood is not good. Unfortunately, our flesh is strong and difficult to train, so we need to ask Jesus to help us.

We talked earlier about an attitude of gratitude. When we are grateful for what the Lord has done for us, we will be in a better mood. I am very thankful for the husband God gave me and how he works to provide for us. Have you thanked your husband lately for something he has done for you and your family? My pastor says that men are an ego wrapped up in flesh. Thanking our husbands and praising them is like saying *sick'em* to a bull dog. They will do everything they can to please us and gain our acceptance and appreciation. We want our homes to be a place our husband wants to come home to, our children want to bring their friends to, and friends and family love to visit. Our homes should be a little piece of Heaven on earth.

Many times we are so burdened down with the tasks at hand we forget to check our mood and attitude. As a working wife and mother, I fully understand the tasks a woman faces each day. For many years I went to bed at night and mourned the tasks that went undone. I lived my life in arrears; there was always something **past due**. I usually set myself up for failure. Do you do that? I would always have my to-do list overloaded with more than was possible to be achieved in one day. This is when our responsibilities turn into burdens. My zealousness was to check off my list. One thing about household duties, they are never done! I began to pray that the Lord would help me cut away the chaff or the unimportant stuff. *Casting all your care upon him; for he careth for you.* (1 Peter 5:7) Unimportant tasks are those things that just do not matter in the whole scheme of things. One example of this would be putting up a new wreath on the front door, when the children have sports and homework that day. Or doing my nails when the laundry is piled high and no one has clean underwear.

We go through many phases and seasons in life. When children are small, things are crazy. As they get older, responsibilities change, but the schedule is still tight. We need to focus on things that are important in light of our current situation in life. I am a fanatical house cleaner! An unclean house drives me to eat! One thing that helped me in this area was to keep the dishes done and the house straight. I would not withstand the white glove inspection many times, but the house always had the appearance of cleanliness. As long as the house has some semblance of order, I can handle it. I know I can always do the underneath cleaning at another time. Do not forget the involvement of children in the teamwork of taking care of the home.

I also started asking the Lord to help me put at the top of the list the most important tasks. *The steps of a good man* (or woman) *are ordered by the Lord: and he delighteth in his way.* (Psalm 37:23) The Lord showed me that God's order of priority is: God, husband, children, home, and then everything else.

That they (the older women) *may teach the young women to be sober* (sound mind), *to love their husbands, to love their children, to be discreet, chaste, keepers at home, good, obedient to their own husbands, that the word of God be not blasphemed.* (Titus 2:4-5)

I found that once I lined up my tasks and priorities with God's order, everything seemed to flow much better and to fall into place. Finally, but most importantly, I started going to bed each night thanking the Lord for what I had gotten done that day. I counted my blessings instead of my undone tasks. I just want to praise the Lord because He truly transformed my life in this area of stressing over duties.

When a woman works outside of the home, juggling all of her responsibilities can be quite an ordeal. In my personal experience, it has been difficult for me to handle all of my responsibilities and fulfill the role that God called me to be, as a wife and mother, while working fulltime. That is not to say that a woman who does not work outside of the home has less responsibilities. The real difference is that one has more time than the other to take care of the tasks for her home and family. I have heard much preaching, teaching, and discussion over the years about Christian women working outside the home. Ultimately, it is up to the husband whether a wife works outside the home. *For the husband is the head of the wife, even as Christ is the head of the church.* (Ephesians 5:23a) If a husband requires his wife to work, as is my case, she should comply. If a husband does not want his wife to work, she should not.

Titus admonishes the older women to teach the younger women to be *keepers at home.* (Titus 2:5) We already learned that the word keeper means to be *a guard and a stayer at home*. One of the responsibilities of a guard is to not leave their post. We know that the virtuous woman in Proverbs 31 worked with her hands and *perceiveth that her merchandise is good.* (Proverbs 31:18a) Merchandise is generally items sold for a profit. From all indications it seems that the virtuous woman of Proverbs 31 was a keeper at home with a home based business. I should also add that the Proverbs woman had many servants to help with her tasks, which women do not have today.

I have been very fortunate to work from home the majority of my work life; however, I still missed a lot with my children during their growing up years. A woman can be very creative and cost effective when she applies herself. If your husband desires for you to work outside the home, there can be alternatives with his permission. My daughter is a stay at home mom, a coupon queen, and a consultant for two individually sold product lines. Ladies, we can do whatever task is set before us, but only with the Lord's help. We do the best we can and leave the rest to the Lord.

All of this instruction sounds good except for those who may live in homes where the husband is not saved or is not living for the Lord. An unsaved husband and a husband that is not walking with the Lord often behave about the same. Also, a husband who is a newly saved Christian may not yet know how to lead his home in God's way. I mentioned previously that my husband was saved seventeen years after I was saved. For most, like myself, an unsaved husband does not necessarily mean an unpleasant home life. Often husbands will not take the leadership position in their homes as they should.

A young woman mentioned to me that her husband would not lead in the home and nothing she did helped. I told her something that you may find odd. I told her to pretend he was leading. One meaning for the word pretend is *imaginary*. Imagine that your husband is leading or go through the motions as if he is. Go about your life in all manner as if he is leading. Continually bring matters before him to decide. Pray and look forward to the day he will lead as he should.

On the old television show, Green Acres, one man held several jobs. The man would appear at the post office window with his uniform on and in the next moment he would appear behind the counter of the general store with a different uniform. Our husband holds the position of leadership whether he performs it or not. *For the husband is the head of the wife, even as Christ is the head of the church.* (Ephesians 5:23a) As with any position of authority, when responsibilities are neglected others have to pick up the slack. The others are us! Act as if he is leading and do whatever is necessary until he leads. Our job is to honor and submit to our husband's authority or position, no matter what. Sometimes we may have to put on his uniform for a moment in time, with meekness, not usurping his wishes. We know our husbands and what makes them tick. We generally know what they want done and how.

Finally, there are homes where home life is unpleasant or even horrid because of the husband's leadership and behavior. Some men can be brutish and very overbearing. Pray to the Lord God of Heaven who can change the situation. *The king's heart is in the hand of the Lord, as the rivers of water: he turneth it whithersoever he will.* (Proverbs 21:1) If physical abuse occurs, seek immediate help from your pastor.

In Our Church

As Christians, we should be members and participants in a local church. Together in Christ, a local body of believers draws strength, encouragement, and spiritual training from their fellowship. Our number one responsibility in our church is to be in attendance. *Not forsaking the assembling of ourselves together, as the manner of some is; but exhorting one another: and so much more, as ye see the day approaching.* (Hebrews 10:25) As wives, we have most of the responsibility for seeing that our family is prepared and ready to go to church. If our husbands do not go, we should still go and take the children. Sunday can be a very hectic day. We need to start preparing on Saturday to be ready for Sunday. A home where Christ is at the center will also have Sunday at its center. Do not forget the mid-week service as well! Church is where we go to hear the preaching and teaching of God's Word and to be with fellow believers. Every service God prepares a meal from His Word to be delivered by the pastor to us. Preaching and teaching are *profitable for doctrine, for reproof, for correction, for instruction in righteousness.* (2 Timothy 3:16b) *Those that be planted in the house of the Lord shall flourish in the courts of our God.* (Psalm 92:13) We need to be faithful to God's house.

When we are not involved and participating in our local church, the church deteriorates. Our church should be a lighthouse in our community drawing people to the Savior. The physical church structures are not the church; the church is the Christians that make up the church body. If we are not faithful to church services we are in sin, according to Hebrews 10:25; we are neglecting God and His house. Extra church functions and activities, outreach programs, and church work are very important and vital to the church body. We need to be as faithful as we can to these times, especially outreach ministries. Reaching out to the unsaved is the life blood of Jesus Christ.

After I was saved, I jumped right in and started serving the Lord in my church. I taught Sunday school, served as church secretary, and led vacation Bible school. I did all I could do in serving. I thought that was what I should do. All of my serving was good, but a detriment to my unsaved husband. Often we do good things for the Lord, but not the best. *Behold, to obey is better than sacrifice.* (1 Samuel 15:22b) I was not following God's order of priorities in my life. The Lord was merciful to show me the error of my ways; and with His help, I slowly started to get things in order and put my husband in the proper place in my life.

This meant I had to back off of many of my church duties. Many people in my church could not understand this. I took some criticism, even from church leaders. Through this time the Lord taught me something about judging others and their situations. *Judge not, that ye be not judged.* (Matthew 7:1) Some of the meanings for the word judge in this passage are *to decide, conclude, determine, or to call in question.* Often it is easy to identify sin in a person's life by the Scriptures. However, we cannot know how the Lord is leading or dealing with others in their lives concerning their walk with the Lord. Ladies, be very mindful of your husband in the area of church activities and added church responsibilities. Before my husband was saved, I chose to miss many extracurricular church activities, because I was leaving my husband at home alone too often. Although, I did make sure I was faithful to every church service.

We were created to glorify God in our lives, witness to the lost, and encourage other believers. Our faithfulness to God's house is an encouragement to our pastor and fellow members. When folks participate together in a worship service, they are saying to each other, "This is important to me and I am for this." When we do not show up for a service, others think church is not important.

In addition to being faithful, we need to encourage others. Women should encourage other women. What exactly should we encourage other women about? The disciples went from city to city checking on the believers *and exhorting them to continue in the faith.* (Acts 14:22b) We need to encourage others to continue in the faith. We also encourage others to walk this Christian walk or live their lives according to how Jesus instructs. *Furthermore then we beseech you, brethren, and exhort you by the Lord Jesus, that as ye have received of us how ye ought to walk and to please God, so ye would abound more and more.* (1 Thessalonians 4:1) The word encourage means *to inspire, to boost, to cheer.*

When we see others in our church struggling, we need to come alongside them and encourage them in the Lord. *Now we exhort you, brethren, warn them that are unruly, comfort the feebleminded, support the weak, be patient toward all men.* (1 Thessalonians 5:14) Unfortunately, what often happens in our churches is we destroy the struggling and the weak ones. We destroy a person's spirit when we admonish and correct without love and compassion. We destroy a person's spirit, when we misjudge situations. We destroy a person's spirit, when we repeat words and information we should not be repeating. We destroy a person's spirit, when we avoid them or withdraw from them because they don't *walk* like we do. We destroy a person's spirit, when we act with a *holier than thou* attitude. Any one of us could be on the receiving end of the destruction at any time. The battle against Christians is very strong today. The work of the Lord is monumental, and we cannot and should not be killing our own army!

There are those times when we do have to withdraw from a brother or sister who has been lovingly admonished, but refuses to turn from sin. However, in too many situations we are misjudging. We do not know people's lives like the Lord does. Only the Lord knows what a person has to deal with each day, the hardships they face, and the intensity of their temptations. We need to show love and compassion every opportunity we get. We also need to create opportunities to show love.

I would like to suggest some ways we women can encourage other women. First, we can pray for our sisters in Christ every chance we get. Often it is good to let them know we are praying. In these days of texting and messaging, it is very easy to send a quick word of encouragement. Next, befriend the loners and those who do not seem to fit in. Over the years of being a Christian, I have seen so many slip into church, come for a while, and never seem to connect with anyone. The next time I look around they are gone. Often it is the individual's own choice to move in and out, but sometimes a friendly face, a kind word, or hug can open a world of difference.

I remember a lovely red-haired woman that came to our church many years ago. For a short time she would come in and sit on the back row; she looked lonely. I tried to talk with her a couple of times. One Saturday morning, I was reading the obituaries and her name was there. She had just been in church the previous Sunday and the pastor had visited on Tuesday. Later that Tuesday, she took her own life and left behind a small baby, a son, and a husband. I was horrified and could not help but think we could have somehow made a difference in her life. She professed to know the Lord, but obviously was struggling.

We need to be alert and conscious of our fellow believers. Care about the concerns of others. *A word fitly spoken is like apples of gold in pictures of silver.* (Proverbs 25:11) A kind word, a sweet note, a text, or a phone call can carry a lot of weight. When you have the opportunity, prepare a meal or even just one dish for someone going through a difficult time. Provide Scripture verses that apply to situations someone is dealing with. Visit the person's home. We need to pray and ask the Lord to lead us in what we can personally do to help others.

Losing visitors and members to death is a sad time for a church. It is sad for those of us suffering the loss, but good for those who graduate into Heaven. Even more difficult is the loss of members in other ways. My hometown of Charleston, South Carolina can be described in one way as a college town. We have many folks that come to Charleston to attend the Medical University of South Carolina. My home church benefits greatly from people coming to Charleston for school. We have gotten many couples over the years that come to church with us during their college term. Most of these couples have been well seasoned Christians who jump right in and serve the Lord with us. We have benefited greatly from the talents and abilities of these individuals. We grow friendships with these folks and are always sad to see them leave.

Unfortunately, we also lose members when people fall away from the Lord and stop coming to church. I can think of people right now that I served alongside that are completely out of church. This is one phenomena that has always puzzled me. I guess my greatest concern for these folks that I love is their eternal security. Only the Lord knows where they truly stand with Him. The verse that often comes to my mind in these situations is found in 1 John 2:19.

They went out from us, but they were not of us; for if they had been of us, they would no doubt have continued with us: but they went out, that they might be made manifest that they were not all of us.

The worst loss to endure in a church, I think, is a loss that results from a church conflict. A few years ago our church suffered a great loss of about 60 people. For a church with an average attendance of 180 at the time, that is a major loss. I only mention this because I think it is very important for Christian women to know their jurisdiction and influence during a church conflict. If I had to state in a few words what caused this problem in our church, it would be a power struggle that was a result of setting men up above the Lord. We needed a purging, but no purging is ever easy.

And I will purge out from among you the rebels, and them that transgress against me: I will bring them forth out of the country where they sojourn, and they shall not enter the land of Israel: and ye shall know that I am the Lord. (Ezekiel 20:38)

The land of Israel symbolizes being under God's rule and His prosperity. This verse in Ezekiel was truly lived out in our church. When there is a church-wide conflict, it puts brother against brother and sister against sister. Many choose a side and it is not always the Lord's side. My husband was a fairly new deacon during this time, as well as a fairly new Christian. I have to say this situation was the most difficult situation we have endured yet as a Christian couple. Even as I recall this experience, the tears swell in my eyes. It is the job of men to fight wars and solve conflict, not women. The Scripture is filled with situations of conflict dealt with by men led by the Lord. I learned so much from the Lord during those difficult days. The most important lesson was silence.

If there ever is a time in church where we women should be silent, it is during church conflict. Women often talk to lay out facts and to reason or understand situations. Often we talk just to gossip. We never have all of the facts. It is not our place to understand all of the details in a church conflict; it is for those who need to resolve the conflict. There is a reason why leadership meets behind closed doors and the discussions are confidential. All of the facts cannot be published for many reasons. We live in an information overloaded society and we think we need to know everything so we can make our own personal judgments. *There is one lawgiver, who is able to save and to destroy: who art thou that judgest another?* (James 4:12) During our silence we need to stay on our knees before the Lord. *The Lord shall fight for you, and ye shall hold your peace.* (Exodus 14:14) Pray for every part of the situation; pray for the men who are dealing with the conflict; pray for the church body to be preserved; pray for the conflict to be resolved quickly with the Lord glorified. Unfortunately, war and conflict are never without casualties. Pray for the wounded, those who have stumbled, and even for those spiritually dead. Only the Lord can set things right again in a church and heal the members.

In the World

When we come to know Christ as our Savior, we also become foreigners or strangers to the lost world. The way foreigners are identified is generally through their speech and their appearance. *But ye are a chosen generation, a royal priesthood, an holy nation, a peculiar people.* (1 Peter 2:9a) People generally see us or hear us before they know us. The word *peculiar* in 1 Peter 2:9 means *purchased or possessed* (of the Lord). Our dress and presentation should look like we have been purchased and belong to our owner, Jesus Christ. We should always be modest, neat, and appropriate in our dress for the setting. Unsaved folks should see something different about us.

Our speech needs to be God-honoring and pleasing to Him at all times. Our speech needs to be different or foreign to those around us. Dressing and speaking like the world will never set us apart for the work of Christ. I wonder if a lost person could pick us out of a crowd. I know one family that found a Christian lady in the frozen food department because she had on a skirt instead of beach apparel like most of the other shoppers. The world expects a lot from those who call themselves Christians. Once a person knows us, their identification of us as Christians should be confirmed. How? Mainly by seeing our love for them and others. *By this shall all men know that ye are my disciples, if ye have love one to another.* (John 13:35) Christians are confirmed to be Christians by their love for each other and their love for the lost world.

Christians should also be identified by their behavior. I once had a business meeting with an elderly lawyer. He commented that there was a day in this country where lawyers could hold their heads high and be proud of their profession. However, that day had long passed. I feel his comment could very well apply to Christians. Professing to be a Christian at one time meant something. The world once knew and expected that Christians behaved in a certain way, but not so today. I have heard people in business say that Christians are the worst for paying their debts. That ought not to be so. *See then that ye walk circumspectly, not as fools, but as wise.* (Ephesians 5:15) *Circumspectly* means *diligently and perfectly*. As much as is possible, we need to walk upright in this world. We need to be diligent in all we do, honest in our speech and business transactions.

Our main responsibility to the world or the unsaved is to tell them about Christ. We should love unsaved people as Christ does. *For God so loved the world, that he gave his only begotten Son, that whosoever believeth in him should not perish, but have everlasting life.* (John 3:16) The person that loves lost souls has a heart very near the heart of Christ. All we do for the lost is an outpouring of our love for them to see them saved. We need to minister to the unsaved like we minister to our fellow Christians. We need to love, care, and do what we can to help the lost. *As we have therefore opportunity, let us do good unto all men, especially unto them who are of the household of faith.* (Galatians 6:10)

We need to witness every chance we get and often we need to make the chances. I do not know about you, but I have a hard time directing my conversations with the lost toward spiritual matters. It is easier with family and friends, but more difficult with strangers. I can give out tracts all day long, but I believe a personal word goes a long way. I have asked the Lord to help me be bolder to ask the point blank question: If you died today, do you know if you would go to Heaven? I believe I miss many opportunities. I also believe that time is very short before the Lord comes back.

We live in this world, but we are not part of it. We need to witness to the lost, but be very mindful of the influence the lost world can have on us and our walk with Christ. The more we are involved in the world and **hang** with the world, the more the world will witness to us and conform us. *Be not deceived: evil communications corrupt good manners.* (1 Corinthians 15:33) Friendship with the world is enmity with God. *Love not the world, neither the things that are in the world. If any man love the world, the love of the Father is not in him.* (1 John 2:15) Satan loves for Christians to walk close to the world for two reasons: 1. Worldly Christians are hard to identify as Christians and are very ineffective for Christ. 2. When we walk close to the world it is very easy to fall into the sin, practices, and beliefs of the world.

As women, our very best friends should not be unsaved. Friends who are not saved are never going to point us to or influence us for Christ, His Word, or His ways. Once we are saved we should not have much in common with lost friends. God's Spirit living in us, after salvation, will not identify with the spirit of an unsaved person. What we see, hear, and do will determine who we are for Christ. As for the lost world, we need to love them, care for them, and strive to see them saved.

Conclusion

A Christian woman's sphere of influence is greater than she will ever realize while she is on this earth. As women it is vital to know how we fit into and function in that sphere. Obviously the most important place of influence is in our home. We have an awesome opportunity to serve the Lord in our homes and make them a haven of godly learning, blessings, and rest for our families. As we guard and build our homes, we are not just taking care of today's duties and responsibilities. We are building for a lifetime and future generations. What is sown today will produce many times over in our children, grandchildren, and great-grandchildren. What we build today in our homes will impact those outside of our homes as well, such as family, friends, fellow church members, and the lost world. The influence I desire to make most is to lead lost souls to the Savior and encourage the saved to walk close to Him. The poet C.T. Studd says it best in his poem entitled *Only One Life*. Here is the first stanza.

Two little lines I heard one day,
Traveling along life's busy way,

Bringing conviction to my heart,
And from my mind would not depart,

Only one life, 'twill soon be past,
Only what's done for Christ will last.

Chapter 5 Review

1.   What is the most important decision we can ever make in our life? (Romans 10:13)

2.   We are body, soul, and mind. What does Scripture say about our body after we are saved? (See 1 Corinthians 6:19-20)

3.   Name the most important thing you think a woman should do to take care of her body.

4.   The first thing we need to do to take care of ourselves spiritually is to take an inventory and see where we need to improve. How do we do this? (See 2 Corinthians 13:5 and Psalm 51)

5.   To keep our emotions in check we need to have a sound mind. How can we have a sound mind? (2 Corinthians 10:3-5)

6.   In Chapter 4 we learned that our home needs to be centered on _____.

7.   Who should be the head of our homes? (Ephesians 5:22-23)

8.   How does a woman set the tone in her home? (1 Peter 3:4)

9.   Is there a verse in the Bible that forbids women to work outside the home?

10.   Women need to prioritize their responsibilities. Titus 2:4-5 gives the priorities in order. Can you name them?

11. What is the most important job we have in our church? (Hebrews 3:13)

12. List ways we can encourage others in our church.

13. List jobs a woman can do in her church.

14. When trouble or turmoil comes to our church, what is the best thing for a woman to do about it?

15. What does Scripture say about us (Christians) and the world? (1 John 2:15-16)

16. Name our number one job or responsibility to the world (unsaved)? (Matthew 28:19-20)

17. Should a Christian woman have very best friends that are unsaved? (James 4:4)

18. What kind of issues could result when we have best friends that are not saved?

19. How can we show the love of Christ to the unsaved?

Chapter 6

The Evening of Life

In this our final chapter, we discuss the final years of life. The idea for this entire study guide was birthed in the topics we will discuss here. In fact, my original idea was an entire book on these matters. In June of 2013, my 99 year old grandmother fell and broke her hip. She had been able to live alone up to that age, by the grace of God. In the days after her fall, a scenario unfolded that I am sure happens on a daily basis all over the world—the dilemma of where and how to care for an aging parent. I am sure you will understand when I say that much discussion and some family politics ensued concerning this dilemma.

Up until the time Grandma broke her hip, her daughters and granddaughters were all very active in her life. Only a couple of these caregivers know the Lord. When it came time to make important decisions about the rest of Grandma's life, seniority left some of us out of the decision making process. One daughter actually separated from the other siblings during this time. Children and grandchildren do not think the same way concerning grandparents and their care. They both see things from a different perspective, and indeed they should, because they have a different relational basis.

In the weeks that followed Grandma's accident and the resulting life changes for her, I did a lot of thinking. I sat back, watched behavior, listened to different reasoning, and I contemplated much.

As a Christian, I wanted to be sure I handled this situation in a way that the Lord would have me to. When exterior family conflicts arise and many of the participants do not know the Lord, chaos can ensue. Christians can easily get right in the thick of things, if we are not careful. I love my grandmother very much and I have always been very passionate about how older people are treated. I feel the American culture is pushing older folks to the curb. I also feel we have a responsibility to take care of our elderly. It was not difficult during this time to think ahead, to when I would reach a place that my children would have to deal with these issues for me.

Growing Old Gracefully

We all know that growing older is not an easy process. When we are young, we wish that time would move quickly so we can reach adulthood. Once we reach adulthood, we wish we could turn back the clock! This is especially true when we hit those golden years. Or is it the grey years? The year I turned 30 was by far the worst year of my life, or at least it seemed that way at the time. The whole issue was my attitude. I felt that 30 was the top of the hill and the other side was just a slide straight down. I went kicking and screaming. I did not even want to tell my age. I declared I would be 29 plus for the rest of my life. I never even contemplated that things could get worst. The year I turned 40 my body began to fall apart! I developed a leaking blood vessel in my eye from Macular Degeneration and got arthritis in my foot. The eye doctor told me I had the eyes of a 60 year old woman. Happy birthday to me!! I thank the Lord that both issues were resolved. At 50 the hot flashes came, burning up one minute and cold the next. I cannot wait to see what age 60 brings!

My age change traumas seem pretty funny now, but I think they demonstrate a truth in a lot of people's lives. The truth is we go with the flow and look for what the Lord has ahead for us; or we scoff and complain, fighting it all the way. Those who do not fight the trip are generally much sweeter to be around. I pray for sweetness every day! Growing old gracefully means to grow old with poise, style, charm, and kindness. *Though our outward man perish, yet the inward man is renewed day by day.* (2 Corinthians 4:16b) As Christians, when our inward man is renewed every day and we steadily mature in Christ, we will be sweet senior saints. The following are the *be*-attitudes of growing old gracefully.

Be healthy. In Chapter 5, we discussed taking care of ourselves in all areas, but only touched lightly on physical health. What we sow physically in our youth, we will reap in our old age. I know the debate exists as to whether our physical infirmities are due to genetics or life style. However, we all know that life style has physical consequences. *Be not deceived; God is not mocked: for whatsoever a man soweth, that shall he also reap. For he that soweth to his flesh shall of the flesh reap corruption.* (Galatians 6:7-8a) Sowing to our flesh means participating in the sinful works of the flesh. However, it can also be applied to how we treat our physical fleshly bodies.

We have medical facts that show us that smoking leads to lung cancer. My dad died at 57 from lung cancer. He smoked from a teenager until his death. We have medical facts that drug use leads to early death. In my lifetime, I have seen two young adults die of heart attacks after years of drug abuse. I can certainly testify to reaping what I have sown in my own physical life. I mentioned earlier about my years of fretting and anxiousness; well, that leads to stomach troubles. At this stage of my life, I am suffering the consequences of stress with daily stomach issues and the inability to eat the foods I love. Not only does stress have physical consequences, overeating does as well. I am a woman raised in the south and I love to cook and eat. Food is the means by which we nourish our bodies to live, not the reason we live. *And put a knife to thy throat, if thou be a man given to appetite.* (Proverbs 23:2)

Overeating leads to extra weight on our bodies. As women age, the ability to lose weight lessens. Our metabolism changes and slows with age. We need to be fit and maintain the weight that is appropriate for our frame and our structure. Excess weight causes our bodies to work harder to function. We also need to stay active. Our Christian sisters in the first century lived longer. There are two things that contributed to their longevity: food and exercise. The food consumed in the first century was freshly grown and cultivated, not processed or filled with chemicals. In addition, food quantity was less prevalent. The mode of transportation was commonly two feet. The work and labor was more strenuous, which kept folks more active. There was no television or forms of entertainment that resulted in a sedimentary life style.

Get up and get out into the fresh air; go on walks. Eat well to live well. Drink plenty of water. Keep your mind sharp. Read good books, especially the best book—the Bible. Deep study of God's Word helps keep the mind active. Play word and number games. Keep up with world news. There will be times when disease or ailment comes that we cannot prevent. We do the best we can and work through it—do not just lay down and die. Pray and leave the rest to the Lord.

Be gracious, which means to be kind, pleasant, and polite. The word gracious is an adjective (a descriptive word) derived from the word grace. I hope people can describe me as gracious. We often explain grace as not getting what we deserve. A gracious person does not give to others what is deserved. As maturing Christian women, we should be progressively behaving more and more like our Savior. Our Lord Jesus Christ shows us how to be gracious, because He is gracious with His unconditional love and kindness.

Jesus answered and said unto her (woman at the well), *if thou knewest the gift of God, and who it is that saith to thee, give me to drink; thou wouldest have asked him, and he would have given thee living water.* (John 4:10)

Most Christian ladies (myself included) probably would have avoided the woman at the well. Nonetheless, Jesus did not avoid her. He loved her enough to give her the Gospel. When we love others unconditionally, we always consider them first. Jesus is gracious in His forgiveness. All we have to do is ask and He forgives and forgets our sin. *When Jesus saw their faith, he said unto the sick of the palsy, Son, thy sins be forgiven thee.* (Mark 2:5) When we forgive others as Jesus did, we can be gracious to them.

Jesus was gracious in His kindness and compassion. *I have compassion on the multitude, because they have now been with me three days, and have nothing to eat.* (Mark 8:2) Compassion for others leads us to graciously care for their physical needs. People followed Jesus everywhere. He never turned anyone away. Gracious people will attract others to themselves, which is a good thing. Then we can point them to the Savior. We need to be telling the lost about Jesus and we need to be encouraging Christians to live for Him.

Be thankful. Thankful women are gracious women. I do not know about you, but I thank the Lord most every morning that I wake up and get out of my bed. I am not quite sure why though, because to depart and be with Him is far better. In my humanness, I want to stick around to be with my husband and my family. I thank the Lord for my home, daily provisions, for my family, and the list goes on. *In everything give thanks: for this is the will of God in Christ Jesus concerning you.* (1 Thessalonians 5:18) We can find something to be thankful for every day of our lives. Our salvation is the greatest gift for which we can be thankful. As we grow older and illness or physical difficulties come, it is a challenge to be thankful; but as we look back over our lives and remember how the Lord has worked and provided, we have so much to be thankful for. Thankfulness overcomes grumbling and complaining.

Every man also to whom God hath given riches and wealth, and hath given him power to eat thereof, and to take his portion, and to rejoice in his labour; this is the gift of God. For he shall not much remember the days of his life; because God answereth him in the joy of his heart. (Ecclesiastes 5:19-20)

Thankfulness is the opposite characteristic of complaining. It is so easy to fall into the habit of complaining all the time, especially as we get older. I often find myself doing this. When I begin to complain in my life, the only thing that helps is rejoicing and counting my blessings. If I am unhappy with someone, I begin to focus on their good qualities. If I am unhappy with a situation, I begin to look for the good parts of it. Try it! It works!

Be humble. Recently a young person was unhappy with me in a business matter. The person had failed to take care of her responsibilities and I did not respond in a good way. I was called to task for my response and I sincerely apologized. Unfortunately, instead of focusing on her actions and taking care of the task at hand, the young person continued to confront me about my actions, which took the spotlight off of her. It is very difficult for an older person to take admonishment from a young person. I must say it took all the strength I had with the Lord's help to respond in a humble manner.

Our Lord was a humble person. He is the creator and ruler of the entire universe. He sets up authority and puts leaders in their positions. Yet when He was questioned and ridiculed in front of an unjust court, He said nothing. *And when he was accused of the chief priests and elders, he answered nothing.* (Matthew 27:12) The world defines humility as having a modest view of our own importance. I submit that a Christian's definition of humility is rooted in the fact that we have no importance. If I am anything or can do anything, it is because of Christ. The Lord God created us and gave us our abilities; we have no sufficiency in and of ourselves. Have you ever noticed that Jesus (God in flesh) always deflected attention and glory to His Heavenly Father? *I can of mine own self do nothing: as I hear, I judge: and my judgment is just; because I seek not mine own will, but the will of the Father which hath sent me.* (John 5:30) What an example to the believer.

Let this mind be in you, which was also in Christ Jesus: Who, being in the form of God, thought it not robbery to be equal with God: But made himself of no reputation, and took upon him the form of a servant, and was made in the likeness of men: And being found in fashion as a man, he humbled himself, and became obedient unto death, even the death of the cross. (Philippians 2:5-8)

Be Fun. I asked the ladies in our Bible study group what one trait they wanted to have when they were older. My pastor's wife answered, "To be fun." I second her recommendation! When I think of fun people, I think of Janet Graziano. Janet and her family were members of our church for a long time and dear friends. Janet is a prankster. A visitor to her home, more times than not, will come in contact with her pranks. The most memorable place in her home to be pranked was the potty room.

On one occasion at a ladies' fellowship, I became a victim, along with several others. This was not the first time I was a victim, so I should have been prepared. While visiting the potty room, I heard a man's voice emit from the toilet when my weight on the seat activated a hidden gadget: "Hey, what are you doing? I am working down here!" Oh, how it made me jump! Of course, laughter followed outside the bathroom door!

Janet always has a smile. She is one of those merry people, who has a contagious happiness that we are drawn to. The ladies at church loved to be around her and hear her stories with her animated facial expressions. Sometimes she had us laughing so hard we were in tears. Laughter is such a good medicine. *A merry heart doeth good like a medicine: but a broken spirit drieth the bones.* (Proverbs 17:22)

It is much more desirous to be around merry, happy people than grumbling, complaining people. As we age we have a lot to share with the younger generation about the Lord and His goodness. They will be more apt to hang around a merry senior citizen. I must say that when the time is appropriate, Janet is as direct at witnessing and encouraging, as she is at being fun. Hopefully, the same will be said of us.

Be planning ahead. I mentioned at the beginning of the chapter that I thought a lot about growing old as I contemplated my grandmother's situation. It is very easy to put thoughts of growing old on a shelf, because we are not really looking forward to that time in our lives. Most people avoid the subject of death and funeral planning. It is very important to think about those days ahead. *The wisdom of the prudent is to understand his way: but the folly of fools is deceit.* (Proverbs 14:8) My thought process was first directed at making sure I do grow old gracefully. I also thought about dealing with family and being gracious when it comes time to depend on others for care. Our willingness to cooperate with others makes the process easier for us and them. We need to be kind and gracious to the family willing to provide care for us.

Another important part of my thought process was making provisions for how I would be cared for. Couples ought to discuss decisions for future care together. As much as possible, parents should plan for and set aside funds for their care in the golden years. Putting the proper legal documents in place is also a must and so helpful for our families. Those documents would include, but are not limited to: a Will, a list of personal items to go to family at our deaths, a Healthcare Power of Attorney, and a Financial Power of Attorney. Writing out our funeral plans and dying wishes is also helpful. The state of South Carolina has a form called *Five Wishes* that is very helpful in taking care of the legal documents needed.

We need to let our children know where all of these documents are stored, as well as other important items. Keeping our clutter and personal possessions in check is also another good plan. When my grandmother had to move out of her home, it took many days for us to clear out 50 years of her life from her home. If we have keepsakes that we want to give to family, we can do it before death. We need to de-clutter as we can and ask for help from the children.

The way I plan for events in life is to go through all the possible steps of what needs to be done or what could happen. Obviously, we cannot anticipate every situation that could occur, but we can consider a good bit. Many of us have come in contact with dealing with major illness and death in some form, which helps us with planning. When the day comes that we have a major illness or we need to be cared for, we will be glad that we gave these matters some forethought.

Be trusting in the Lord. One of our responsibilities as Christians is to trust the Lord every day and in every situation. *For whatsoever is not of faith is sin.* (Romans 14:23b) As we grow older and come to the end of our lives, the Lord will help us through—just as He has our entire lives. We may need Him more in that phase of life than we ever have. I think Psalm 71 must have been written when David was older; the entire chapter seems to speak to an older person. *Cast me not off in the time of old age; forsake me not when my strength faileth.* (Psalm 71:9) *I will go in the strength of the Lord God.* (Psalm 71:16a) When we are old, the Lord will be our strength. My grandmother at 100 years of age cannot really do many things for herself these days. I often think of how difficult that must be to have to depend and trust someone else completely for everything in daily life. I personally think it would be a little scary, unless we have learned to trust the Lord all along the path of life. *What time I am afraid, I will trust in thee.* (Psalm 56:3)

The qualities and characteristics we should exhibit as we grow old gracefully are ones that should be a result of a close walk with the Lord. I will not say they are automatic, because we have to work on and cultivate many of them. Our life goal should be to be a good testimony for the Lord, even in our senior years.

The "M" Word

It has been said that the only things that are sure in life are death and taxes. Well, if you are a woman and you live long enough, you will experience menopause in some form or fashion. *Now Abraham and Sarah were old and well stricken in age; and it ceased to be with Sarah after the manner of women.* (Genesis 18:11) The *manner of women* spoken of in this verse refers to the monthly menstrual cycle that enables a woman to conceive a child. How many women would say **hallelujah** when that cycle ends? I personally think that the time of menopause can be scary for some women because of the body changes. Some women experience a lot of symptoms, while others only a few. If we have no clue as to what to expect, the issues can be alarming. I think it is important to discuss the changes and symptoms.

I asked my grandmother not long ago about the symptoms she experienced during that time in her life and she could not remember any. This may have been because so much time had passed or her symptoms were mild. I think when I reach age 100 I will remember my menopause symptoms, because some are intense, in my opinion. None of the information I share here is intended to be medical advice. We live in a day when we can learn about any topic just by the push of a button. I always recommend that we research and get as much information as possible about physical ailments from reliable sources. I will discuss several symptoms, all of which may not be associated with menopause—some may be age-related, but begin to appear during the time of menopause. I think it is helpful to share our experiences and the aids that we have found. This helps others have some point of reference.

I already mentioned the hot flashes, which are like a wave of heat that comes over the body. Sometimes I feel as if I will pass out, then in a matter of minutes I am very cold. I personally have associated eating sweets or sugar with hot flashes and so has one of my friends. My hot flashes come a few hours after eating a sugary dessert. When I reduce my sugar intake my hot flashes are fewer and less intense. This makes sense to me when we consider that hot flashes can also be a body's response to inflammation. Sugar causes dryness and dryness causes tissue inflammation. Dryness is also a menopause symptom. The medical community insists that hot flashes are a normal result of decreased levels of Estrogen in the female body and are not related to any other medical condition.

According to WebMD.com stress also contributes to hot flashes. Reducing stress can reduce hot flashes. There are over-the-counter vitamin formulas that help prevent or reduce hot flashes as well. Night sweats are extreme hot flashes that occur when sleeping and can cause excessive perspiration. In addition to menopause, there are many other causes of night sweats; some can be serious.

Anxiety and irritability are symptoms of menopause. Our bodies are going through hormonal changes, not the same as during pregnancy, but similar. Emotional highs and lows are very common. I remember thinking one day that I felt so unkind I could spit nails! Each woman is different in which symptoms she deals with and to what intensity. It is senseless to suffer intense menopause issues and not seek medical help. Often a doctor will prescribe hormone replacement therapy and/or some sort of anxiety or mood altering medications. In my situation, hormone replacement therapy increased my blood pressure. There are women's clinics that exist for the sole purpose of aiding women dealing with menopause related issues. It is between a woman, the Lord, her husband, and her doctor as to what path she chooses to aid with menopause symptoms. As Christian women, we need not judge another's course of action. One good note is that many menopause symptoms will pass or lessen with age.

Two troubling signs that I experience may or may not be menopause related. One is a lessening ability to multi-task. When we are young, we can pay the bills, cook supper, and help a child with homework all at the same time. I think the Lord gives women the ability to multi-task because of all the responsibilities. However, now at the age of 55 I really have to concentrate or focus more on what I am doing. Also, when I get deep into thought about something, I can do things and really not remember that I have done them. This makes me think of people who sleep walk!

The other sign is the inability to remember something right on the tip of my tongue! The forgetfulness that resulted from too much busyness in our youth often increases with age. I have seen women from age 33 to 73 hunting for their cell phone, while it was in their hand—or their glasses, while they were on their head! To some these types of changes can be very frightening. I have often wondered if I have early Alzheimer's disease or am I losing my mind. I talk to many women who think the same way. It is important to know that one key indicator of Alzheimer's is forgetting what things are used for—such as not knowing what to do with a phone. Another clue is substituting different names for objects, such as calling the phone a hair brush. One thing is very certain, there is a lot of information available and we have no excuse to remain in the dark about the changes we face as we age.

Leaving a Legacy

Many people associate a legacy with an inheritance or valuables left to someone at death. The word legacy involves much more than just money and valuables. Sadly, the unsaved world would prefer the legacy of money and valuables, but that should not be the case for Christians. To me a legacy should last much longer than any earthly valuable. I think a legacy should continue for generations. God's Word endures through all generations. *For the Lord is good; his mercy is everlasting; and his truth endureth to all generations.* (Psalm 100:5) Money and valuables will perish, but the eternal soul will live somewhere forever. The greatest legacy any of us can leave to another is to lead them to Christ through God's Word. We do not give them salvation, but we introduce them to the One who does. *For what is a man profited, if he shall gain the whole world, and lose his own soul? Or what shall a man give in exchange for his soul?* (Matthew 16:26) What better legacy to leave for others than the gift of eternal life? What better legacy to leave than a life in which our God provides everything a person needs?

I mentioned in Chapter 5 that a Christian's number one responsibility is to share the Gospel with others. We need to be soul conscious every day of our lives. I have to admit that it is so easy for me to go about my business and forget to witness or hand out a Gospel tract. I also have to admit that even after being saved for a long time, I am still nervous about speaking to others about Christ or deciding how to start the conversation. I do make a point to carry Gospel tracts with me at all times. I put them in my wallet, so every time I pull my wallet out I see them. One thing that seems to make witnessing easier is when I use myself as an example. I ask a person how their day is going and then respond, "My day has been great; the Lord has really blessed or answered prayer." When a person is dealing with an issue, I can tell them how the Lord worked in my life in a particular situation. *But sanctify the Lord God in your hearts: and be ready always to give an answer to every man that asketh you a reason of the hope that is in you with meekness and fear.* (1 Peter 3:15) We do not have to wait for someone to ask us about the hope we have; we can find ways to insert it into a conversation. If I start with my experience with the Lord or my testimony, it opens the door.

Spring is just arriving as I write this last chapter. There is just something about this time of the year that makes most people want to get out in the yard and plant. The other day I purchased Sunflower seeds for my grandson, because he expressed an interest in planting. When I handed him the package of seeds, he ran around the house shaking the package, exclaiming "I need to grow something!" We Christians all need to grow other Christians. The Lord Jesus used many planting illustrations in his teachings. We need to plant the seed of the Gospel and hopefully lead it to germination. When we plant a seed and it sprouts, we do not just walk away from it. We have to care for young plants and get them to a mature state, even if we did not plant the seed. The same goes for us as Christians.

Not only are we to plant, we are to nurture. *And the things that thou hast heard of me among many witnesses, the same commit thou to faithful men, who shall be able to teach others also.* (2 Timothy 2:2) The word *faithful* in this verse refers to believing men or other Christians. When we nurture and encourage a young Christian we leave a legacy—a legacy of Christians who will witness to others and encourage other believers. There should be a continuous cycle of planting and growing other Christians.

As we grow older and mature in Christ, we need to encourage believers in the things we have learned. *But speak thou the things which become sound doctrine.* (Titus 2:1) We need to be an example before them. *But be thou an example of the believers, in word, in conversation* (actions), *in charity, in spirit, in faith, in purity.* (1 Timothy 4:12b) Paul wrote this to young Timothy in the ministry, but it also applies to maturing, older Christians. Encouragement, reinforcement, and inspiration have no age limit. New believers need the most attention, but Christians of all ages need encouragement and help along the way. This includes ourselves.

We need to teach believers to love God and to put Him first. *Jesus said unto him, thou shalt love the Lord thy God with all thy heart, and with all thy soul, and with all thy mind. This is the first and great commandment.* (Matthew 22:37-38)

We need to teach believers that God can be trusted. *Our fathers trusted in thee: they trusted, and thou didst deliver them. They cried unto thee, and were delivered: they trusted in thee, and were not confounded.* (Psalm 22:4-5) Can we put ourselves in this verse? Have we trusted in the Lord and been delivered? We need to relay that to others.

We also need to teach believers that God is faithful. *Know therefore that the Lord thy God, he is God, the faithful God, which keepeth covenant and mercy with them that love him and keep his commandments to a thousand generations.* (Deuteronomy 7:9) What a lasting legacy we have in our Lord God.

There is no better place to start and leave a legacy than in our own families with our children and grandchildren. We have a responsibility as parents to plant the seeds of God's Word and water them in our children. Hopefully, we will be the ones to lead them to the Lord. As grandparents, we should aid our children through prayer and encouragement, as they seek the salvation of our grandchildren and walk the Christian life. As parents and grandparents, we should be a living testimony, in word and deed before our families. For generations the people of Israel passed down the legacy of faith in God and His Word by mouth. One generation told the next. We Christians do not seem to do that much anymore. God and who He is should be brought to life in real stories. I know we have the complete Word of God, but we also need to talk about Him. The psalmist reminds us:

Give ear, O my people, to my law: incline your ears to the words of my mouth. I will open my mouth in a parable: I will utter dark sayings of old: Which we have heard and known, and our fathers have told us. We will not hide them from their children, shewing to the generation to come the praises of the Lord, and his strength, and his wonderful works that he hath done. That the generation to come might know them, even the children which should be born; who should arise and declare them to their children: that they might set their hope in God, and not forget the works of God, but keep his commandments. (Psalm 78:1-4 and 6-7)

Oh, what a legacy we have in Christ. We need to continually show that legacy forth in our life in word and deed. One day we will leave this earth. My sincere prayer is that when I am gone my family and fellow believers will say: *She knew and loved the Lord. She was faithful. She cared about me. She pointed me to the Savior. She encouraged me to follow the Lord and to be a better Christian.* Amen. What do you want people to say about you?

Caring for Our Elderly

As we discuss caring for the elderly, the most important point I want to establish is that we are responsible as children for our elderly parents. *But if any provide not for his own, and specially for those of his own house, he hath denied the faith, and is worse than an infidel.* (1 Timothy 5:8) The word infidel refers to a *non-believer.* Our own house includes more than just our spouse and children—it also includes our parents. I know this because the main topic of 1 Timothy Chapter 5 is the care for widows or women who have lost their husbands to death. Often widows are those in the greatest need of care.

A Christian that will not care for those of his own house is worse than the unsaved. *But if any widow have children or nephews, let them learn first to shew piety at home, and to requite their parents: for that is good and acceptable before God.* (1 Timothy 5:4) *To requite* means *to give or do something* for the parent, as if giving back for all they have done for us. *Honour thy father and thy mother: that thy days may be long upon the land which the Lord thy God giveth thee.* (Exodus 20:12) The word *honor* means *to attach a value to a person, respect them, or to hold them in high regard.* In the world today, elderly people are not valued as they should be. Nursing homes are full of elderly parents that are dropped at the door and only visited a few times a year, if ever. As Christians, our care for our elderly parents should be much different from that of the world. Care for the widows is not the responsibility of the church, unless a widow has no family or the family will not take care of their obligation. *Pure religion and undefiled before God and the Father is this, to visit the fatherless and widows in their affliction, and to keep himself unspotted from the world.* (James 1:27)

How we approach the responsibility of caring for elderly parents is an individual family matter. A solution for one is not a solution for all. When the time comes, I personally plan to care for my mother in my home, if I am physically able. I am not a huge fan of nursing homes, although sometimes they are necessary. When an elderly parent is disabled and in need of extensive nursing care, there may be no other alternative than a nursing home. I remember a lady who had to place her elderly brother in a home, but she went every day and fed him lunch. There are solutions that will work for every situation, with the Lord's help.

A husband and wife should decide together how to approach their particular situation. Consulting with doctors, home health workers, and other caregivers always supplies us with good information. There are many dynamics involved with elder care. If there are other siblings, elder care becomes a group decision. A group of siblings joining together to care for a parent can be a very good situation or a very bad situation. Unfortunately, very few families are complete with all Christian members always behaving as they should. A group discussion or decision on the care for an elderly parent can often become a family argument. We, individually with the Lord's help, will have to determine how we fit into an unruly family situation. *If it be possible, as much as lieth in you, live peaceably with all men.* (Romans 12:18) No matter how difficult or uncivil a family situation becomes, we can never shirk our responsibility to our elderly parent.

I have often thought of the challenges for those in full-time Christian service to fulfil the responsibility to care for a parent. I have a friend with two sisters and they each take a year caring for their invalid mother. My friend and one sister have husbands who are pastors. If the full-time ministry is stateside in a church, arranging care for a parent will be easier. I have an unmarried friend who is in full-time ministry and she is willing to move her ministry to be closer to her aging parents when the time comes. However, for missionaries on a foreign field the challenge to aid parents has to be great. The Lord knows the hearts of His people and He will guide them in what they need to do when the time comes. He can also provide help in other forms when necessary. Those who set out to honor their parents and care for them as they should, will be helped by the Lord in their situations.

As a grandchild it was difficult for me to not have a say in the outcome of my grandmother's care when she had to leave her home. We are very close and I had been assisting her in taking her places, some household responsibilities, cooking, and getting items from the store. In my confusion as to what my role was, I talked to a retired pastor who gave some advice I think will be helpful for many. Pastor Wade Bostic told me that I needed to submit to those in authority over me. I was stunned for a moment, not expecting that answer. He further explained that children were first in line in the decision process concerning a parent, not grandchildren. That thought never occurred to me, although I have seen families that submit to elders for authority. Many families defer to the eldest child for direction in family decisions about parents. It is also very appropriate to defer to husbands and male siblings, no matter the age, for decisions about parent care. If families would acknowledge and follow a chain of command, many times it would alleviate family problems.

Do not forget the emotional aspect of elder care. It is difficult to see our parents very ill or declining in health and mental status. It can also be difficult for the parent to age and deal with what the Lord has for them in their last days. Family emotions involved in major decisions concerning a parent always add another dimension to the situation.

However we approach the care of our parents, it will be a challenging situation. When Dad or Mom get to the stage that they need help, it is not easy for anyone. Once it is settled where the parent will live, there are adjustments for everyone. When we take an elderly parent into our home to care for, our lives will change, as well as theirs. Our living space, our time, and our resources all have a different focus. A person who takes on the care of another really gives up his or her life. My grandmother ended up going to live with my cousin, Vicki Miller, and her husband and daughter. Vicki describes taking Grandma home, like bringing a new baby home; but they did not have nine months to prepare the space and make it safe for an elderly person with a broken hip.

Looking after a person 24 hours a day is very tiring. There are also a lot of duties and needs to attend to, some of which are not pleasant. In certain situations, elderly parents cannot do anything for themselves. The caregiver then is responsible for all duties and the actual caring for the parent. A caregiver will encounter situations they never thought of before. Vicki pointed out that an elderly person's skin is fragile and easily damaged. A simple bath can leave an injury. Like bringing home a new baby, there are no instructions that will help with all elder care involves. Patience will be needed in great amounts.

No matter who the parent goes to live with, every family member can help in some way. Some examples of things that can be done: go sit with the parent and relieve the caregiver, make meals, do shopping, do errands for the caregiver and the parent, take the parent to medical appointments, help clean the caregiver's house, send funds when needed, etc. The list is endless of the things we can do to help in the situation with an elderly parent or grandparent. A lot of these same tasks may need to be done for parents even before they have to leave their homes. Karen Powell, my pastor's wife, told me that her mother cared for three elderly family members at different times when Karen was young. She said these were some of her mother's most difficult days. Caring for the elderly is difficult. There is no guilt or shame in making that statement. Just because it is difficult does not mean we do not want to do it. We love our parents and grandparents. Even with the great difficulty of caring for the aged, it is rewarding to give them good care and see them through their final days.

I have only discussed elder care until now from the aspect of the children or caregivers. How does the parent fit into this discussion?

The parent is actually the most important part of this discussion and that is why I saved them for last. Even though a parent comes to the point that they need care, they are still our parents. We need to respect their wishes and desires as much as we possibly can when they are able to express them. We need to always be respectful and honoring of them. We need to keep their dignity intact. We need to care for them and protect them from harm. There will be times when we have to make tough decisions and our parents will not agree. We need to listen to their concerns, their suggestions and desires, and comply when we can. When we cannot comply with their wishes, we need to provide good sound direction and plans, always keeping the parent in the loop.

Obviously, if Mom is 90 and can barely see, she should not be driving. I remember a dear Christian lady that should not have been driving. She was in a bad accident in which her automobile was totaled. Fortunately, she was unharmed. She insisted on continuing to drive. My husband was her mechanic and she had him looking to replace the wrecked car. The family asked him to stall and not replace the car. The lady's memory was not good and failing every day. Poor thing, she called him for months asking if he had found a car yet.

Just this week, someone made this statement to me, "Mom just won't listen." I have heard that comment so many times and my usual response is, "As a parent, I guess I wouldn't want my children telling me what to do either." *Rebuke* (chastise) *not an elder.* (1 Timothy 5:1a) It goes against the grain of a parent for a child to tell them what to do. It is unnatural to them and it should be. Our parents have been our parents all of our lives; when they get to the point that they need our care and assistance, they do not want us bossing them around. You may think that statement just does not apply to every situation, but it does. I have worked with and helped several older people and have not found one yet that wants to be told what to do by their children.

I have made some interesting observations about seniors that are well worth mentioning.

- Mothers are far more likely to take direction from their sons or son-in-laws than their daughters.

- When we make suggestions and explore all of the possibilities with them, parents are more willing to negotiate.

- Parents do not want to be kept in the dark about the plans we are making for them.

- Parents have a difficult time leaving familiar things and places.

- When parents get older, they tend to cling to the child or caregiver that is with them and helps them the most, even to the exclusion of other children. One reason for this is that elder parents do lapse into an insecure stage just like children.

- People who are sick or helpless and cannot care for themselves will lean on the one they think will be there for them. I have seen this many times.

- What we see as stubbornness in an elderly parent is their way of maintaining some control in their lives.

- Familiar settings and habits give an elderly person a more secure feeling.

I really cannot close this section without addressing the finances of an elderly parent. As a bookkeeper, my contact with elderly clients has always started in the realm of their finances. I am sure you can imagine I have seen good, bad, and ugly in this area. It is unimaginable to me that many children feel that what is their parents is also theirs. I think that is indicative of the generation we live in that believes they are entitled to everything. *For the love of money is the root of all evil: which while some coveted after, they have erred from the faith, and pierced themselves through with many sorrows.* (1 Timothy 6:10) Obviously the matter of money can be a source of family conflict while caring for the elderly and after their death. A pastor told me once that there is always controversy in families over money, even Christian families. Please remember that what other family members do or do not do, does not relieve us of our responsibilities to care for our parents. Care includes physical, emotional, spiritual, and financial provision.

A good process to follow when caring for the finances of a parent is to have accountability. This needs to start in the very beginning of the care, because as time passes family members can be more defensive about accountability. Often caregivers feel they deserve access to a parent's money because they are giving the care. When one person handles the finances alone, there is more room for misappropriation, error, and questions from other family members. *Abstain from all appearance of evil.* (1 Thessalonians 5:22) Accountability can be achieved by allowing someone else to sign checks, review the check register, and bank statements. All of the parent's assets such as cash, automobiles, and property, etc. needs to be handled in an open and up front manner.

Conclusion

Thinking about aging and the changes that will come is not appealing to anyone. However, unless we die young, we will all face the challenges of aging. I have found in my life when I am not thinking and just moving along with life, my actions and my words are dictated by my emotions and my situations. As a Christian woman, I need to be thinking, planning, and being led by the Lord as I age. *I press toward the mark for the prize of the high calling of God in Christ Jesus.* (Philippians 3:14) We need to live the best life we can on this earth, which takes forethought and the Lord's leading, not happenstance. We want to finish this race well for our Lord.

In addition, we will have to deal with the aging of our parents. Contemplating our parents getting older and losing physical and mental abilities is very saddening. Unfortunately, it is a fact of life. But just like any trip in life, we need to plan ahead and think about how we will handle it—to make the trip easier for all of the travelers.

Chapter 6 Review

1. Have you thought much about aging? Name one goal you have in order to age gracefully.

2. Read Proverbs 16:31 and write what you think it means.

3. Can you think of one factor that determines whether an elderly person will have a good disposition?

4. Typically when we see grey or white hair we think someone should be wise. What makes a person wise in God's eyes? Can you give a verse?

5. Can you name any of the physical, mental, or emotional aspects of menopause?

6. Define the word legacy.

7. What is the most important legacy we can leave in any person's life?

8. The next important legacy we can leave is? (See Deuteronomy 4:10)

9. How can a grandparent leave a legacy in a grandchild's life? (See 2 Timothy 1:5)

10. In today's society we have a growing issue with honoring parents and the elderly. What does it mean to honor?

11. Do we ever get to an age where we can stop honoring our parents?

12. Read 1 Timothy Chapter 5 and explain what the Scripture says about caring for the elderly.

13. 1 Timothy 5:1 speaks about not rebuking an elder, what does that mean to you?

14. What age group would be an elder?

Epilogue

The material in this study guide stems from the lessons the Lord has taught me over the past 28 years of knowing Him as my Savior. I learned even more as I studied the Scriptures and put this information together. I tried to be very transparent, so you could learn from my many mistakes. The transparency of others always helps our lives because we learn that we are not alone in the similar situations we face. The Lord wonderfully created a theme throughout the chapters of this book that I hope you discovered. The common theme is knowing the Lord, trusting the Lord, and staying in His Word. Ladies, we cannot live this life without Him.

I sincerely hope the Lord revealed some things that will strengthen your walk with Him. Anytime we hear or read teaching on the Scriptures and the Lord's will for our lives we have a choice to make. The choice is to do something with what we have learned or walk away unchanged. James says that when we walk away unchanged, it is like looking at our face in a mirror and not cleaning the dirty spot we found. However, if we hear and do the Word we will be blessed.

But be ye doers of the word, and not hearers only, deceiving your own selves. For if any be a hearer of the word, and not a doer, he is like unto a man beholding his natural face in a glass: for he beholdeth himself, and goeth his way, and straightway forgetteth what manner of man he was. But whoso looketh into the perfect law of liberty, and continueth therein, he being not a forgetful hearer, but a doer of the work, this man shall be blessed in his deed. (James 1:22-24)

Ladies, it is easy to work on one area of our lives at a time. Begin today to work on the main issue the Lord laid on your heart as you studied this material. May the Lord richly bless you as you seek to serve Him. If you have any questions or comments, please email me: *elainemichele2013@gmail.com*

CPSIA information can be obtained at www.ICGtesting.com
Printed in the USA
LVOW04s0507110914

403404LV00001B/3/P